KISHO KUROKAWA

KISHO KUROKAWA
THE ARCHITECTURE OF SYMBIOSIS

INTRODUCTION BY
FRANÇOIS CHASLIN

RIZZOLI
NEW YORK

First published in the United States of America in 1988 by
RIZZOLI INTERNATIONAL PUBLICATIONS, INC.
597 Fifth Avenue, New York, NY 10017

Library of Congress Cataloguing-in-Publication Data

Kurokawa, Kisho, 1934–
   Kisho Kurokawa : the architecture of symbiosis,
1979–1987.

   1. Kurokawa, Kisho, 1934–   2. Architecture,
Modern 20th century Japan.   3. Metabolism
in architecture (Movement)   I. Title.
NA1559.K82A35   1988   720'.92'4   87–43253
ISBN 0–8478–0909–9 (pbk.)

Original title Kisho Kurokawa Architecture de la symbiose 1979–1987
first published in France in 1987 by Electa Moniteur.

Introductory texts by François Chaslin translated by Richard Miller
Designed by Richard Medioni
Text layout by Blackpool Design
Printed and bound in the U.S.A.

6

François Chaslin

The itinerary of Kisho Kurokawa is that of an entire generation, for most of the great Japanese architects experienced a similar evolution. In the past they went their separate way, somehow apart from the rest of us, stubbornly expressing their modernist message, impatient heirs to the powerful brutalism of Kenzo Tange, engaged in the daring futurist speculations of metabolism. It was something of a golden age, a rare moment in which architectural thinking merged with the aspirations of a society violently caught up in the problems and the intoxication of growth. And now today they seem to be cropping up all over the world, building everywhere, though not without having considerably smoothed their rough edges and adopted a highly fluid strategy that has enabled them to move easily in the world of international business and politics with immense competence, whether it be in Singapore or in Düsseldorf.

Kisho Kurokawa, the former "child prodigy," now seems to have parted ways with mechanics. The man who burst vividly upon the scene around 1960 by playing a major role in the creation of the metabolist movement seems today to be entertaining more tranquil notions, less futuristic, more imprecise, more ambiguous—notions of "symbiosis," to use his term, that are dominated by an often delicate and refined realism, one mindful of tradition, perhaps even a bit too versatile.

And where is this man going, this man who is always in a hurry, this transcontinental architect who is forever between planes, constantly traversing hemispheres the way most people go from one room to another? What does he dream about, if dream he still does, with his hundred or hundred and fifty employees, his main office, his branches in Sofia, Tripoli, Abu Dhabi, and perhaps tomorrow Paris, with his meticulous organization that seems to leave no second of his time to chance?

How can he control the conception and execution of such a huge number of projects, sit down to dinner with the world-famous, and then go back to work again at his drawing board? How can he visit work sites scattered across various continents, act as host of a weekly television show on NHK, publish countless books, reviews, essays, and volumes of woodcuts? How can he cast works in bronze, conceive and oversee the execution of elegantly perfect pieces of furniture, and give solid academic lectures with rigorous dissertations on everything from Aristotle to ancient Indian Buddhism?

In all that whirlpool of deeds and ideas, with all those brief nights—almost "as short as those of Napoleon"—and all the back-and-forth time changes, with all those mysterious pills he removes from their box at the end of each meal, how can he continue to be so alert, so precise, so concentrated, a bit tense, perhaps, but always fresh, impeccable, neatly attired in his sober suits, so perfectly courteous and kind, without ever showing either fatigue or emotion?

An impressively efficient machine, a great figure in the business of international architecture, he has forged an extreme impassivity, diluting almost to nonexistence the image of the artist that he most certainly is. It was Charles Jencks who once said that rather than a real, live human being, Kurokawa seemed to him to be a "statistic dreamed up by the Japanese Chamber of Commerce."

And his work is still of a high standard. Relatively removed from fashion and the currents of the day, although one senses the shadow of their influence, his work proffers no catchy or well-articulated doctrine as a rallying point for the regiments of students whose eagerness for theories and axioms to cling to in this period of excessively diverse and changing models is being voiced daily. They may well be misled by work that reveals so little theory, that is so supple, so often chameleon-like, so very adaptable.

For Kisho Kurokawa has travelled thousands of miles from his futurist meanderings of the past. He has abandoned the utopian helicoidal cities, the prefabricated capsules of the 1960s, the spatial excrescences of his pavilions for the Osaka World's Fair, the Sputnik clusters, and the white units, as transportable as huge refrigerators, of the famous Nakagin Capsule Tower. He has abandoned his search for that highly technologized kind of design according to which a dwelling must be as modern and as coolly elegant as an electric razor, as precisely and painstakingly assembled as an automobile.

As early as 1976, with the creation of the Sony Tower at Osaka, a building whose functionalist aesthetic attempted to imitate the fully achieved design of that period's industrial

8 objects, the various elements of the building—the steel boxes for each floor's washrooms simply grafted onto one of the facades, the glass tubes for the elevators, and the oblique treatment of the escalators—were little more than figuration and mere simulacra of technicity and mobility, things that we already knew were illusory.

The metabolist movement conceived of the city as a living organism undergoing a process of renewal and obsolescence, experiencing cyclical transformations, turgidities, and declines comparable to those of organic tissue. Against the usual concept of modern architecture, deemed too mechanistic, it favored an approach to urban phenomena inspired by biology, tinged with Buddhist philosophy, and overwhelmingly trustful of modernity and technology.

Kisho Kurokawa's new doctrine is a more fluid one. With its hints of nostalgia and historicism, it is openly attentive to subtle ideas, to half-tones. It models itself on a rich, austere gray tonality, one that was fashionable during the Edo period: Rikyu gray, "replete with meanings and suggestions and, at the same time, with tranquility." Extremely popular in Japan during the second half of the seventeenth century, the ambivalent color, close to anthracite, was for years the symbol of a certain aesthetic ideal, a "chic" based on wealth and sobriety. It has nothing to do with our traditional notion of the gray created by mixing white and black, but reflects, we are told, the search for conscious, willed austerity, the rejection of sensuality; and it combines various colors "in such a way that they cancel each other out."

Thus, Kurokawa invites us to enter his work by making a detour toward the sensorial and the discrete meanings of forms. Here, too, he seems on the verge of going off into a theoretical universe far more conceptual than ours, one in which the role of emotion is barely touched upon, rarely explicit. Indeed, although Kurokawa's theory sometimes seems faintly artificial, although it appears not to precede and guide his work but to straggle after it, like an a posteriori justification, it still manages to translate by and large the ambience surrounding his creations, at least their least eclectic elements.

Many of his works have a great beauty of surface, texture, and materials. Consider, for example, the Ishikawa Cultural Center, black, hard, with its flowing and recoiling horizontal curves, its steel acroteria, its immense walls squared with shadow, its raw granite plinths; or the Suita-shi National Ethnological Museum at Osaka, with its full, dark, grainy skin, its shiny sheet-metal and glass sheathing, its obvious geometry, and its rigorous detail. Here we have two buildings that are introverted and shut-in, buildings that create a feeling of rocky solidity and strong structure, paradoxically almost contradicting the Buddhist spiritualism the architect promotes, an ideal that seems to concern the transitory nature of things and the sympathy they should arouse in the spirit. However, they are two buildings consonant with the search for an aesthetic of gray, the "tenebrous color" Junichiro Tanizaki described in his 1933 text *In Praise of Shadows* in an attempt to express his feelings of "uneasiness" about the brutal fluctuations between two civilizations.

And perhaps this is what moves us most in Kurokawa's work today: the way he combines the aesthetic leanings of Western modernity and the Japanese taste for opacity, for the depths of dark lacquers, for the "mystery of the shadows," for the play of caressing light reflected off varnished walls, for the cold gleam of wet stones beneath a low gray sky.

We are also pleased by the facades, which, like mighty screens, lend majesty to the passage from the outside to the inside, a progressive transition from the public to the private, evoking for one last time the spatial interpenetration of which the contemporary Japanese city is bereft. We can see this quality revived in several of his projects, particularly in the Saitama Prefectural Museum of Modern Art, whose high cement grill is reflected in a curving glass facade, and in the delicate Shoto Club in Tokyo, which is covered with small white squares that give it an almost misty softness despite its strict geometry.

Yet, that having been said, there are too many other things that the catch-all concept of "symbiosis" cannot mold into a unified representation: a gigantic hotel in Bulgaria, incongruous with its "authentic Japanese garden," wooden houses, and hill

dwellings; a tea house that is a jumble of the *shoin* and *sukiya* styles, exceptionally well executed; a huge scallop like a Royal Dutch Shell symbol for a vast conference hall at Abu Dhabi; a graceful moderno-traditionalist project for a new town in Libya; some baroque undulations à la Aalto here and there. Baroque—a key word now for Kisho Kurokawa, one he applies even to his utopian helicoidal cities of yesteryear and one he seems to feel can account for all the ambiguities, all the double meanings, all the mixed pleasures he continues to insist are legitimate.

So we find him reemploying historical motifs at the Red Cross headquarters, with its vast, pompous interiors; we find curved, Chinese-style eaves and doorknobs at the National Bunraku Theater; we find an incredible stylistic mixture in the Wacoal Kojimachi Building, whose overall exterior appearance is that of a vast machine, while inside it contains composite sites, like the reception hall the architect has described as a "spaceship with Japanese décor": windows with astrological themes, four-lobed false skylights topping columns with mirrored capitals, traditional consoles around partition walls, a mannerist doorway drawn from Italian motifs...

And the Niigata headquarters of Yoshiundo, the manufacturer of religious products, is equally odd, equally composite and capricious. All of these projects are uniquely different, projecting the impression of a maquette or a child's toy: the densely packed half-arena at Nîmes, with its concentric spaces rising like stadium seats; the Japanese Studies Institute at Thammasat University, its regular white structure evocative of a model built of matchsticks, its gables as naïve as something made with building blocks; or the strange Koshi Kaikan, with its bizarre proportions, its collection of curvilinear forms, its fat, round chimney, and the surprised expression of its twin gables.

Kurokawa is evolving along with contemporary world society. He is changing, oscillating. In his quest to mix old and new, in his desire (which we trust is more than merely commercial) to create a "new internationalism," in which regional cultures can somehow intercommunicate under the wing of Japanese Buddhism, and in which the local elements striving to prevail in the face of modern Western universality can coexist, he is moving toward a boundless eclecticism. However, it may be a mistake to regard as Oriental or Japanese the values of symbiosis, of fusing opposites, of ambiguity and tolerance for contradiction, values that are hallmarks of postmodernism everywhere.

The extraordinary and unsettling virtue of Japanese architecture is its ability to lend itself to all interpretations: it inspired both the curvilinear langours of Art Nouveau and the asceticism of rationalism, the immaterial spirit of easy, normalized standardization and the massive and sculptural expressivity of the archaic and raw brutalists. For a century now, the country has been for the West a source of diverse and ever-fresh inspiration; in return, it has absorbed all sorts of imported models without ever abandoning a paradoxical yet deeply felt fidelity to its own national traditions.

THE ARCHITECTURE OF SYMBIOSIS

Kisho Kurokawa

If Japanese culture were to be described in a single word, I would call it "symbiotic." This fundamental aspect of Japanese culture played a most important role in the rapid development of the country.

Since the seventh century, Japan has been deeply influenced by other cultures, including those of such neighboring countries as China and Korea and, through them, those of Persia and Western Europe. The objects in the eighth-century Shosoin, a treasury for the art collection of the Imperial Family, clearly reflect those influences. Many of these treasures were brought over the Silk Road through China from India, Assyria, Persia, Turkey, Afghanistan, and even Rome.

This symbiotic coexistence between Japan and other countries has continued ever since. The Japanese have actively continued to assimilate foreign cultures, adapting what they borrow to fit into their own.

Buddhist thought also created a favorable climate for this tendency toward symbiosis. Buddhism teaches the doctrine of *samsara*, or the transmigration of souls, according to which all living things (human beings, animals, and plants) are part of a perpetual cycle of birth and death within the greater web of life. Fundamental to this philosophy is the belief that nothing is permanent, be it nature, man himself, or architecture. Thus the life of architecture, like that of man, belongs to nature and exists within the cycle of transmigration. It is from these principles that symbiosis emerged and became an established part of Japanese culture.

In 1958, some thirty years after the CIAM (International Congress of Modern Architecture) movement got its start, modernism began to undergo great changes. Team 10, a new group initiated by the British architect Peter Smithson and the Dutch architects Aldo van Eyck and J. B. Bakema, proposed a complete revision of the theories of modern architecture. In 1961, together with the Englishman James Stirling, the Italian Giancarlo de Carlo, and the American Christopher Alexander, I attended a meeting of Team 10 held in Royaumont, France. I still vividly recall the exciting discussions we had about growth, change, identity, and other notions completely lacking in modern architecture.

Around the same time, in 1959, I started the metabolist movement with several other architects. I realized, somewhat vaguely, that Japan was embarking on a path of rapid economic growth and technological progress. If we want to preserve man's identity in an age of such drastic change, I thought, we must first break architecture down into those parts that can change and those that cannot. By so doing, I hoped to prevent whole buildings from being used and then destroyed, like some frail consumer item. If we replaced only those parts amenable to change, the whole building would stand longer, and energy would be saved in the long run. I saw in this kind of control of man over architecture a way of safeguarding man's identity and imparting true humanity to architecture.

The metabolist method distinguishes architectural parts not only according to function but also according to meaning. This differentiation of space on the basis of its meaning makes possible a semiology of architecture. An architectural vocabulary is formed through a combination of "signs" corresponding to autonomous units of meaningful space.

At that time I began research on the technology of prefabrication and the idea of "capsule" architecture, searching for ways to break buildings down into units. I was not only studying the process of mass production but also working toward an architecture capable of growth and change. This architecture was a sort of "self-help system," in that the people living in such buildings could participate in the planning. This is an economically oriented age, an age of big corporations and massive organizations, as well as huge box-shaped buildings and super-high-rises. Under such circumstances, capsule architecture seemed to offer people the restoration of their identity and humanity.

The idea of architecture as a phenomenon that constantly changes with nature and society, rather than as a permanent piece of art, conforms to the Buddhist concept of the impermanence of all things, a traditional part of Japanese culture.

12 Also long established in Japanese thought is the view that technology and man are not in an oppositional relationship but in a symbiotic one, technology being an extension of man.

The metabolist movement also sought to use Japanese cultural traditions to help reconstitute the rules for modern architecture, which had originally been based exclusively on Western ideas. We reaffirmed the value of history, ornamentation, and the vernacular and strove to achieve a symbiosis of past and future. By actively incorporating local distinctions, we asserted the importance of the symbiosis of different cultures.

Over the past twenty-five years, the ideas of symbiosis put forth by the metabolist movement have begun to take root. I would not go so far as to say that modern architecture was wrong in every respect. But if functionalism and rationalism, the main tenets of modern architecture, are applied without discrimination, we end up losing the intermediate spaces between elements of different quality and the valuable ambiguity between areas made distinct by functionalism. The philosophy of symbiosis advocates a reappraisal of these properties of dual or multiple meaning.

In discussing my approach to architecture, let me first explain some of the contradictions and problems inherent in modern architecture. At the risk of oversimplifying, I would attribute the failure of modernism to four major causes: dualism based on function; universalism through industrialization; order by hierarchy; and materialism.

In its most extreme form the dualistic approach classifies architectural and urban spaces solely according to function. The CIAM's famous *Athens Charter* divides cities into spaces for work, spaces for daily living, and spaces for recreation, all joined by traffic arteries. The theory of zoning rests on the concept of analysis by function. Of course, some people objected to this kind of functionalism: for instance, the anthropologist Jan Mukarzowski, of the Prague Constructivist group, was concerned with the vital sources of function and insisted that it was impossible to reduce any human act to a single function. In contrast to the monofunctionalism of Le Corbusier, he advocated multiple functionalism. In spite of such criticism, however, industrialized society and the machine provided the perfect setting for the supremacy of simple functionalism and its analytical approach.

The disordered or jumbled multiplicity of functions that had accumulated over the course of history was seen as antimodern and was thus rejected. Clearly expressed functions, vast open areas, greenery, and fresh air became the bywords. Le Corbusier's *Ville Radieuse* seemed a good way to introduce the fresh air of modernism into cities. Since the time this idea was first proposed, high-rise architecture, open plazas, and greenery have become the dominant urban images, not only in Brasilia and Chandigarh but in contemporary cities everywhere. However, these cities have proven themselves failures in creating human environments. In *Vers une architecture*, Le Corbusier compared meandering roads to "donkey paths" and stated that man's roads should be straight because he has a purpose. To which I respond: To attain their purpose, human beings veer, zigzag, and detour. Thus their paths should never be straight.

The source of functionalism's analytic approach is in the very basis of Western rationalism. If we trace it to its origin, we can follow it back to the architectural thought of the ancient Greeks. In his *Metaphysics*, Aristotle delineates the three principles of beauty: *taxis, symmetria,* and *horismenon. Taxis* means order, a state in which classification has eliminated chaos. *Symmetria* means measured together, indicating division of the whole on the basis of a fixed dimension or volume. *Horismenon* means restriction. For the ancient Greeks, philosophy consisted of first separating things from the reigning chaos and then ordering and restricting them through the application of reason.

The principle of rational selection and division has been the dominant current throughout the history of Western thought. From this has come the constant reliance on thinking in terms of dualities: good and bad gods, the light of god and the darkness of the material world, and the Christian mythico-religious dichotomy between God the creator and his creations. Descartes described the duality of the physical being and the spiritual being. Kant's philosophy of matter and phenomena, or of freedom and predestination, was a further example of dualistic

Roppongi Prince Hotel, Tokyo.

Saitama Prefectural Museum of Modern Art.

thinking. Today, dualism and the analytic approach dominate architectural, urban, and social structures in all industrialized nations.

Functionalism was applied most popularly in zoning theory, and it can be seen in the racial divisions of cities like New York, in the planning of residential districts on the basis of income, or in the designation of town centers as business areas and outlying regions as residential zones. In terms of social welfare policies, functionalism has separated the handicapped and the elderly not only from city centers but also from their communities and families by putting them away in institutions.

In Western society, architecture and the city are in fundamental opposition to nature. Stout walls divide outside from inside, city ramparts clearly establish boundaries between the city and the surrounding natural landscape. In modern, contemporary cities, however, there is a dichotomy between public spaces and privately owned spaces, with no provision for communal ownership.

Modern architecture is characterized by the rejection of the commonplace and of anything redolent of the taste of the masses, as well as a separation from the surrounding society—in other words, exclusiveness. The CIAM movement led by Le Corbusier has occasionally been described as humane, in the idealistic belief that improving architecture could revolutionize society. But, in the long run, modernism developed into purism and exclusivism, rejecting the traditions and human concerns that might have made it attractive to ordinary people.

The principles of analysis and dualism can be viewed from many angles. But in modern architecture they resulted in the abandonment of much that is potentially valuable. Experience has taught us that we must now try to reclaim what has been lost. Modern architecture lacked intermediacy, the quality that enabled virtually inseparable, mutually coexisting elements of function to supplement each other. But because the lives of human beings are filled with unavoidable contradictions, it is only natural that architecture and cities should also contain contradictory elements.

I acknowledge the great significance of modernism and modern architecture, and I believe that the rationalism and functionalism that constitute their fundamental aspects are and will continue to be valid. But I think we should go back and pick up some of the things—the intermediate zones and the allowance for vagueness—that the functionalists cast away.

We need a zoning theory that will accommodate areas of mixed function. We need cities where people of all ethnic backgrounds can live together. We need architecture and cities where handicapped people can live with equal freedom. We need residential areas where the young and the old can live together comfortably. And we need architecture where inside and outside are mutually interpenetrating. This is the philosophy of symbiosis: the symbiosis of architecture and nature; the symbiosis of man and technology; the symbiosis of one culture with other cultures; the symbiosis of past and future; the symbiosis of the vernacular and the purist in art.

Universalism was another cause of failure in modern architecture. Modernization meant industrialization, which, through mass production and the consequent reduction of costs, made machines and industrial products accessible to ordinary people. Industrialization affected the entire world, and the leaders of the modern movement were convinced that the international style would also become universal. Since industrialized products tend to standardization and uniformity, modern architecture, too, could be expected to achieve universality.

But industrialization did not spread over the globe on the force of its own momentum alone. A contributing factor was the idea that modernization was equivalent to Westernization, that Western cultural values were the only valid ones.

Certainly this idea was widespread in Japan after the middle of the nineteenth century, when our nation launched a drive to modernize or, more accurately, to Westernize. The pioneers of Japanese architecture in the Meiji period (1867–1912) debated whether their new architectural style should be drawn from the European Renaissance or the Baroque. In either case, their orientation meant that our architectural legacy from that

16 period consists of copies of Western architecture. That was what the Meiji leaders understood to be modern architecture. Obviously, they were wrong.

The idea that modernization and Westernization are synonymous affected not only architecture but many other areas of Japanese society as well. As long as Westernization and modernization were equated and Western values were held up as the standard, other cultures such as those of Islam, Africa, and our own region of Asia remained undervalued, rejected as unmodern.

The longer modern architecture occupies a central place in modern society, the more evident it becomes that the only way to revitalize it is through invigorating contact with the heterogeneous cultures now forced to the periphery.

I do not necessarily insist on traditionalism or ethnicism as the resolution to the problems of universalism in modern architecture. But I do believe that the time has come for the creation of an "interculturalism" in which the world's cultures, while preserving their identities and the value systems of others, are brought together to mutually influence each other for the production of new, distinctive, individual cultures. I believe it is possible to engage in international dialogue through the medium of local culture; pluralistic cultural criteria are actually being worked out today.

We have already seen that the world's peoples will never adopt a common language such as Esperanto, and that an international style of architecture does not have the capacity to spread throughout the world. We have learned that we can carry on genuine international dialogue only by employing the various languages of each cultural sphere. Only by reaffirming the identity and integrity of each culture can we preserve and sustain true globalism.

Hierarchy as an approach to order, a third cause of the failure of modern architecture, also demands reexamination. In modern architectural thought, structure is given precedence over space, infrastructure over substructure, public space over private space, and the whole over the parts, in what can be described as a pyramidal hierarchical order. The same relations exist between architecture and the spaces encompassing it.

A similar order can be seen throughout industrial society, where the principle of efficiency is supreme. Big science, macrotechnology, and big industry form a massive framework within which all other sectors are assigned gradually descending positions. The preeminence given to the macro-framework in the hierarchy of modern architecture excludes consideration of diversity, humanity, and the subtle responses of subordinate details or parts.

I believe that the concept of nondifferentiation and nonuniformity explained by the noted Japanese Zen Buddhist scholar Daisetz Suzuki can provide some help in overcoming the perils of hierarchy and dualism in architecture. As he describes it, the whole and the parts are mutually inclusive in a condition in which there is neither differentiation nor uniformity. Suzuki called both the individual and the society in which such relations exist examples of the Oriental inseparableness. Aldo van Eyck once said, "The house is a small city, and the city is a large house." This idea coincides exactly with Suzuki's thinking.

The house and the city are of equal value and mutually inclusive. The city and the state are of equal value and mutually inclusive. The individual and society are of equal value and mutually inclusive. In architecture, the details and the whole are of equal value and mutually inclusive.

In an order where largeness of scale takes precedence, we must strive constantly to sustain a mutually inclusive relation between architecture and city, between city and nation, between individuals' grass roots sentiments and society in its entirety, between parts and whole.

Materialism is the fourth cause of failure in modern architecture that requires reconsideration. In industrialized society we have witnessed the establishment of a value system that equates material plenitude with the comfortable life, that associates beauty with the permanence of things. As a result of these characteristics, which have infused modernism and mod-

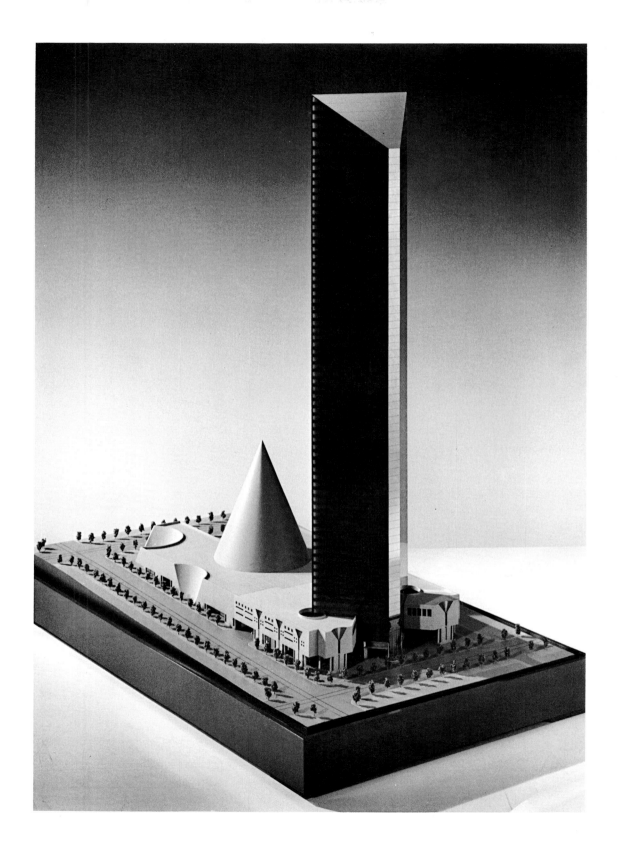

ern architecture, the richness of spirit and the poetic imagery implicit in things and in spaces has inevitably been neglected.

We must restore an appreciation of architecture that manifests the spirit. We must develop our capacity to give free expression to the realm of images. We must recognize and give expression to the beauty of intangible permanence.

As I have said many times, I believe that we can reintroduce some of the important concerns cast aside by modernism and modern architecture by effectively applying suggestions offered by various non-Western cultures.

One of the most interesting of the ideas that can provide a useful paradigm for modern architecture is the doctrine of Consciousness Only. It was advocated by the great Indian philosopher Nagarjuna and is a fundamental undercurrent in Japanese culture. Nagarjuna offers an approach that contrasts sharply with both materialistic and natural/scientific interpretations.

Some years after Nagarjuna's death, around A.D. 300, his thought was compiled into what is called *Samdhinirmocanasutra*, the first written classic of the Consciousness Only school of Buddhist thought. This is not the place to go into a detailed analysis of Buddhist philosophy, but I would like to explain how it has helped to clarify my own ideas on intermediate zones and ambiguity in architecture.

Descartes interpreted matter and spirit as two absolute entities. In contrast, the Consciousness Only school of Buddhist thought sees matter and spirit as manifestations of something more fundamental than either—the storehouse consciousness.

Primitive Buddhism and post-medieval Japanese aesthetics were strongly colored by spiritualism. They gave the spirit precedence over matter and devoted much attention to the creative expression of the transience of the world. The Consciousness Only approach, on the other hand, views both matter and spirit as no more than forms of existence, no more than coded indications of the fundamental storehouse consciousness. In architectural terms, this approach does not emphasize the duality of beauty and function but insists that both are coded mani-

festations of awareness or consciousness. This inspires us to rethink architecture along the lines of semiology or semantics.

The semiology of Ferdinand de Saussure and Roland Barthes is based on a one-to-one correspondence between the sign (the tangible expression) and the intangible referent (the thing alluded to). But as Gilles Deleuze, Félix Guattari, and Jean Baudrillard have shown, contemporary society is replete with signs that have no referent in reality and are essentially meaningless. Expression is born of meaning, but it can also create meaning in its turn. In other words, the sign and the signified are no more than coded manifestations of expression and existence. Function as existence does not substantiate beauty; both beauty and function evoke a sense of space. And behind this is an awareness or consciousness that corresponds to what Jean Baudrillard calls *le poétique*.

In the Consciousness Only philosophy, the realm that is neither mental nor physical, but both, corresponds to what I call an intermediate zone in architecture. This idea is most clearly set forth in the work called *Cheng-weishu-lun*, an ethical evaluation of consciousness that describes an "unimpeding moral neutrality" in relation to acts that are neither good nor bad from a moral viewpoint, allowing a person freedom on the way to enlightenment. This signifies an intermediate approach quite unlike the clear Christian dichotomy between good and evil. The division made is not bipartite but tripartite: good, evil, and neutral. As neutral is neither good nor bad, the superior entity in this philosophy, consciousness, is an intermediate territory. The influence of this Mahayana Buddhist thinking is reflected not only in the qualities of intermediate space, but also in the dual or multiple meanings that apply to numerous phenomena in Japanese culture.

Of course, it is quite possible to find analogous trends in other cultures. I believe, for instance, that the dual meaning and ambiguity characteristic of Japanese culture can be found in Western Europe during the period between the birth of mannerism and the early Baroque. In his *Lo Barroco*, Eugenio d'Ors explains that the Baroque style was the result of conflicting

*Project for the renovation of the area
between Friedrichstrasse and
Charlottenstrasse, Berlin.*

intentions coexisting in one movement. The spirit of the Baroque is the simultaneous wish for affirmation and rejection, the attempt to fly while being pulled down by the force of gravity.

In Correggio's *Noli Me Tangere* (1525), God is shown extending his hand to Mary Magdalene but at the same time refusing to touch her. El Greco's *The Adoration of the Shepherds* (1600) expresses a floating, shifting weightlessness. The Jesuit chapel (1575) designed by Giacomo della Porta has rational and irrational aspects that coexist in symbiosis. Nicolas Poussin, whom d'Ors called the artist of rational passion, demonstrates the symbiotic relation of intellect and emotion in his painting *A Poet's Imagination* (1630), an evocation of motion in stillness.

As these examples show, mannerist and early Baroque art shares the dual meanings and ambiguity found in Japanese culture. As I observed earlier, these are exactly the kinds of qualities that must be reexplored to overcome the inadequacies of functionalism.

Ideas like this can encourage exchange and dialogue between different cultures. I believe it is possible to create a new interculturalism that is totally different from internationalism or the so-called international style.

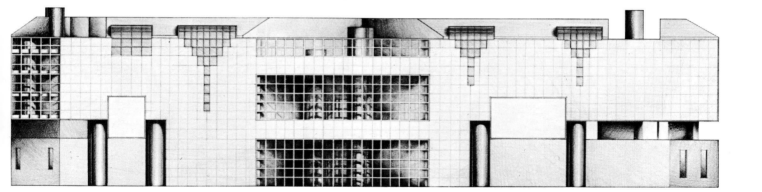

20 Western thinking, and modernist thinking in particular, depends on setting up clear distinctions: black and white, spiritual and physical, inside and outside. A wealth of intermediate nuances is sacrificed to rationality. Indeed, the basis of democracy itself is this kind of dualistic reasoning. We count the ayes and the nays and make a decision based on our tally, even if there is a majority of only one. Such a process seems to thumb its nose at reality. Being aware of the serious flaws in dualist thinking, I have tried to accord a greater importance to the nuances of the intermediate and the transitional.

Around 1962 I became interested in the notion of street architecture, which to my mind ran counter to the Western concept of the public square. From the Greek agora to the Italian Renaissance piazza, Western archetypes have all taken the form of strictly defined, uncovered open spaces surrounded by public buildings. The boundaries of the street are much harder to discern. The constant dialogue between constructions face to face with each other makes the street an undefined area with a temporal dimension, one that changes with the rhythm of human activities, as Jane Jacobs noted. The street is at once an area for traffic, an extension of the intimate universe, and a communal space. Its pluralistic nature gives it a plurality of meanings.

The street is in short a transitional zone where the interior space of individual dwellings meets the exterior space of the public thoroughfare. There is here an interpenetration, a symbiosis, a reciprocal stimulation that carries a considerable affective charge. In *Michi no Kenchiku* (Street Architecture), I explained that this concept of the street was fundamentally Oriental, deriving from an authentically Eastern attitude toward space in general. One could maintain that Western culture is one of stone, whereas Eastern culture is one of wood. Since Roman times, Europeans have built in stone, brick, and earth in order to protect themselves, more from the cold than from the heat. The demarcation between indoors and outdoors is signified by the thick, massive wall. All medieval Italian towns, large and small, had ramparts. The town was within the ramparts, the countryside without. In European architecture interior and exterior are two different worlds. The wall protects the interior from the destructive elements of nature. Fortifications served to defend the town in time of war. The citizenry was within, the enemy without. Thus the wall became an absolute necessity for the community's survival.

There is nothing like this in the Eastern tradition. Vedic texts describe an ideal town whose center holds a "tree of awakening," the medium for communion with the gods. Streets are of two kinds: airy and ventilated for the dry season, light-oriented for the rainy season. Because they were intended as places for the community to assemble, streets became a prolongation of the dwelling space. In the Japanese tradition, space is viewed in the same manner, an attitude reflected in various ways in the architecture. The lattice doors of the houses in Kyoto delimit private property without cutting it off from the outdoors. The verandas (*en*) in *sukiya* architecture are a further

example. At first glance they resemble Western verandas, but they have quite a different function. Common in Japanese working-class dwellings of the Edo period, both in towns and in rural areas, they served as intermediate zones where guests were welcomed amidst the flowers of the garden: they were areas that enhanced contact with the outside. Today, the return to such transitional zones has emerged as a good way of combatting the isolation engendered by modern architecture. The latticed structures of the Saitama Prefectural Museum, for example, or of the Shoto Club are not walls but, rather, linkages with the outside.

To achieve the symbiosis of interior and exterior that I am constantly striving for, I have tried to give as much importance to the interior architecture as to the exterior, to somehow place them on the same level. This has enabled me to reintroduce an expressive dimension that modern architecture had completely neglected in its focus on function alone.

Facade of an urban residence. One's gaze penetrates through the latticework structure into the intermediate zone.

SHOTO CLUB

Tokyo, 1980

22   *Two floors and a basement.*
Roof: *Mortar smoothed with a trowel, asphalt waterproofing.*
Structure: *Reinforced concrete.*
Exterior: *Porcelain tile.*
Fixtures: *Extruded aluminum.*

The traditional Japanese house features such unique spaces as the *engawa*, an enclosed veranda that is neither interior nor exterior but possesses qualities of both; the *nokishita*, a roofed, semi-outdoor passageway; and the *rogi*, a narrow alley between houses in the same block. These special features form an intriguing set of spaces that provide continuity for the occupants and accentuate the symbiosis of indoor and outdoor, of private and public space.

These traditional spaces in modern Japanese cities have become increasingly infrequent due to the prohibitive cost and critical shortage of inhabitable land, as well as to the perpetual noise of urban areas.

This house accommodates a couple (both physicians) and their child. The

North elevation.

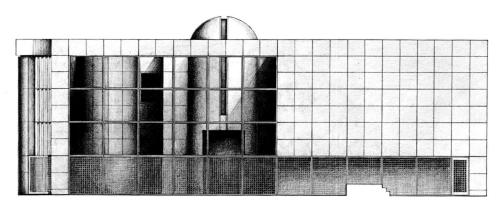

East elevation.

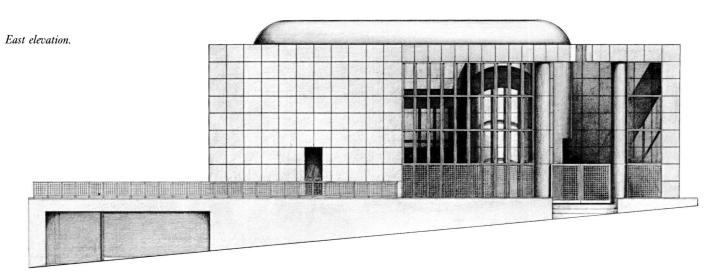

The entryway, showing the intermediate zone created by the facade.

Isometric drawing.

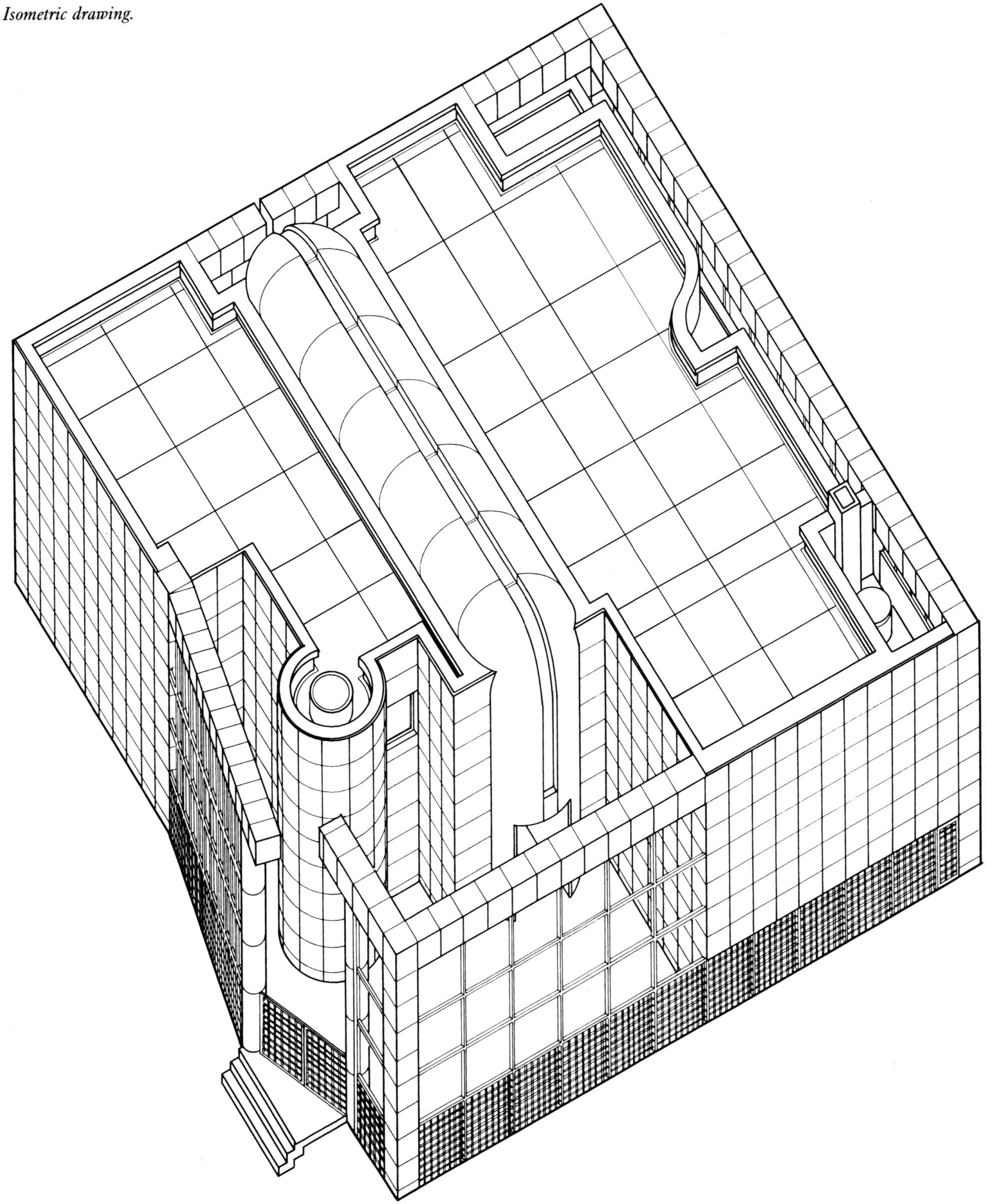

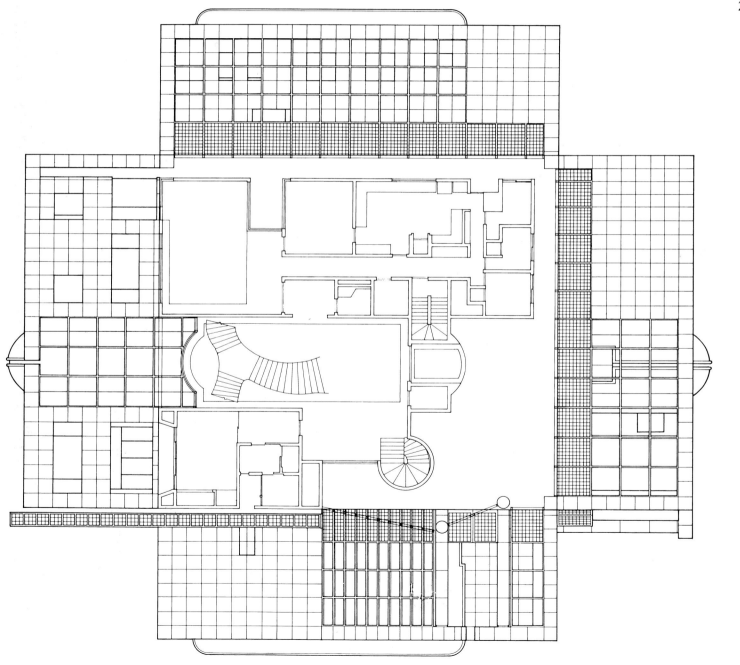

26 ground floor has an entrance hall, a living room, and a dining room, while the upstairs has four rooms. In the basement is a large room for social functions.

Here the attempt was to reestablish spatial continuity by forming new transition zones. The building consists of simple rectangular forms with certain parts cut away from the core. Although some spaces are cut into the building mass, the structure's profile remains. Lattices and framing replace traditional intermediate zones and take on various functions, creating a *roji* (garden) in front of the entrance porch, terraces adjoining private rooms, a screen over the facade of the building, and security fences. The outer lattice wall is open at the entry gate, like a door left ajar, to suggest that visitors are warmly welcomed. The approach to the entrance is indicated by the layout of the stone paving. The interplay of straight and curved lines is continued in the main entrance hall.

Dressing room.

SAITAMA PREFECTURAL MUSEUM OF MODERN ART

Urawa, 1982

30 *Three floors and a basement.*
Structure: *Steel frame partly encased in concrete.*

The overall form of this building is a rectangle, but one side is split in two by a deep cut, while in other sections the walls are recessed. Also, one portion of the facade is projected outward, creating an intermediate space between the latticed exterior wall and the entryway.

Before the main entrance, enclosed within the angled lattice walls, is a spacious garden styled on the inner gardens traditionally located in front of Japanese tea houses. This space serves as a transitional zone between inside and outside, evoking a sense of continuity between the building and its environment.

This page: The latticework on the eastern facade.

Opposite page: The pergola at the entry.

32

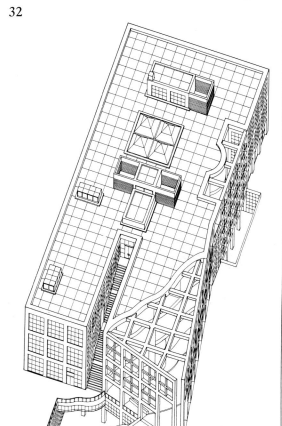

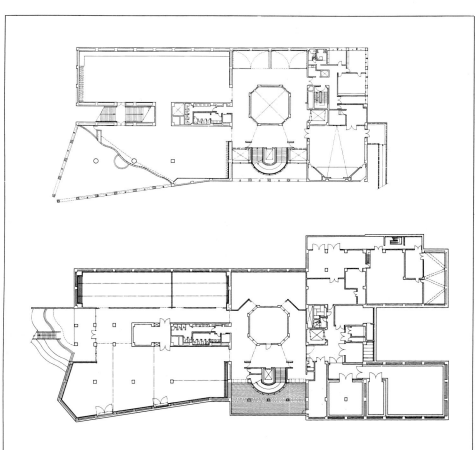

The central space viewed from a side gallery, and the lobby (right).

The skylight of the central space.

34

Below: The lobby.

Bottom left: An exhibition space.

Bottom right: The intermediate zone of the entry.

Nagoya, 1987

36 *Two floors and a basement.*
    Structure: *Steel and reinforced concrete.*
    Exterior: *Aluminum panels and ceramic tiles.*

This museum is situated in Shirakawa Park in the center of Nagoya. The build-ing is oriented on a north-south axis; the western boundary is formed by a beau-tiful tree-lined pedestrian road.

An independent architectural structure consisting of posts, beams, and walls stands in front of the building as a sym-bolic gate and as a site for outdoor ex-hibitions. The large sunken garden and the atrium/lobby that extends it into the basement, beyond a gently curving cur-tain wall, form an intermediate zone that is both exterior and interior. A similar ambiguity characterizes the facade, which is a modern interpretation of traditional Japanese techniques.

General view.

Below: The sunken garden and the entrance.

Bottom: South facade, with pond and sculpture park.

Below: The bridge between the entrance hall and the exhibition hall.

Clockwise from top left: The entry and the sunken garden; the circulation spaces; the library; an exhibition gallery.

38

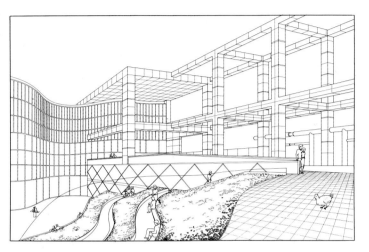

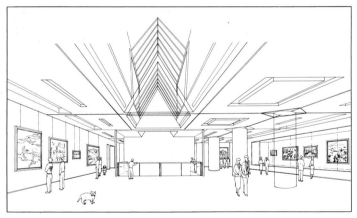

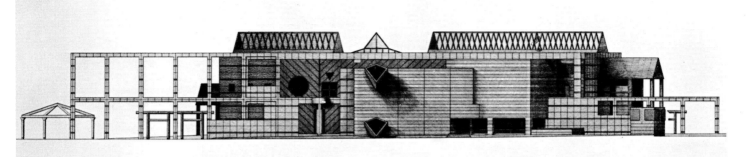

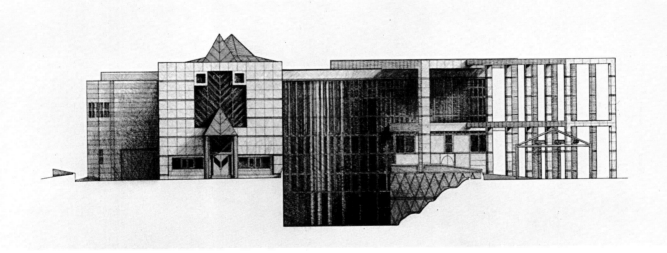

OPÉRA DE LA BASTILLE

Paris International Competition, 1983

40   *Eleven floors, four below grade.*
Structure: *Steel.*

Located in the historical Place de la Bastille in Paris, the new opera house is designed to provide a modern and innovative environment that will contribute to the popularization of the operatic arts.

The glass and aluminum facade of the theater, because of its transparency, encourages an intimate relationship between the public space out front and the foyer inside. The flexibility and dynamism of the design are most evident in the two enormous parallel grid structures that penetrate the site, allowing for outdoor presentations of opera and other performing arts.

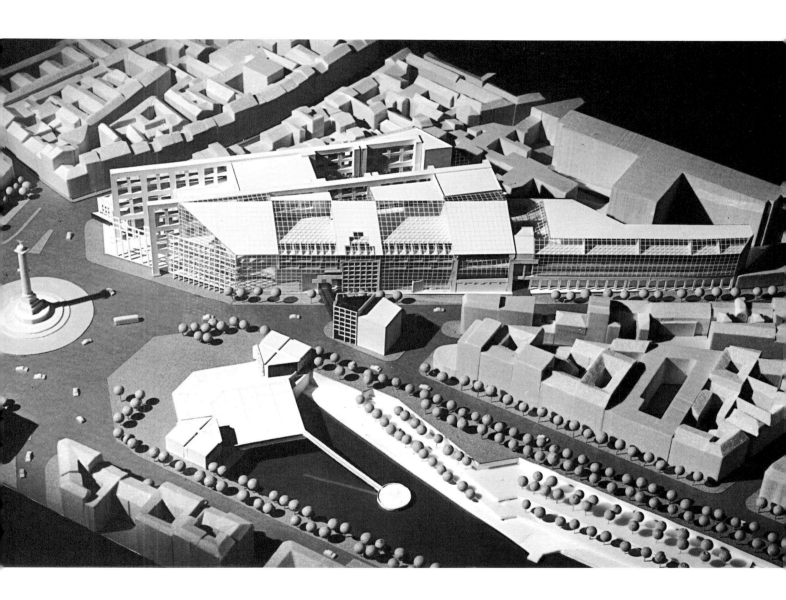

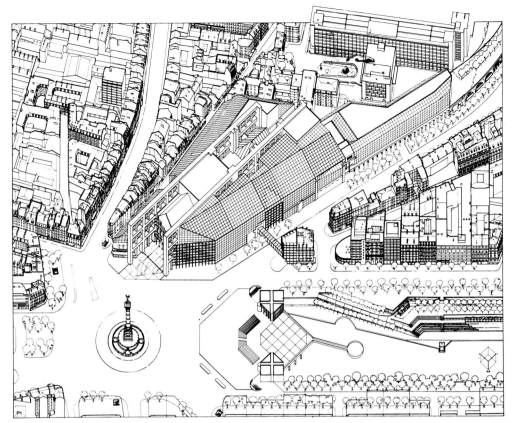

Isometric site plan.

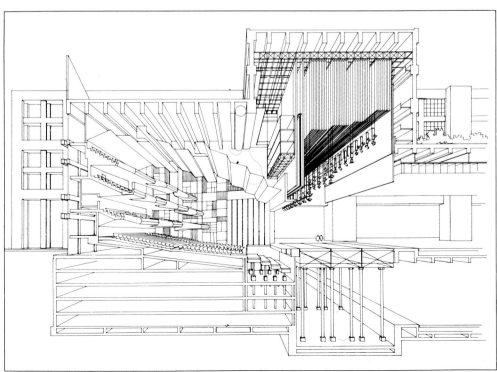

*Longitudinal section
of the theater.*

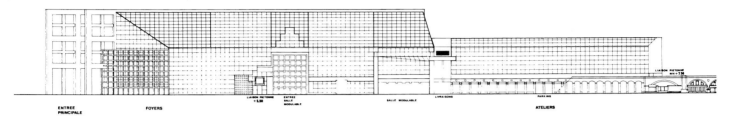

Rue de Lyon elevation.

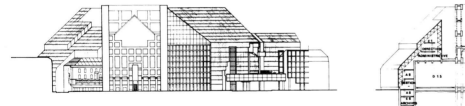

Place de la Bastille elevation.

Transverse section.

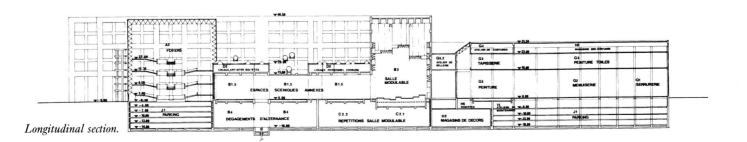

Longitudinal section.

Newport Beach, California, under construction

44   **Structure:** *Steel and reinforced concrete.*

Newport Beach, south of Los Angeles, is California's largest marina and one of the most popular beach resorts in the region.

In the area where the club is located, the view is dominated by the riggings of sailboats, yachts, and ships of all sorts. Thus the notion of suspending the roofs from fourteen masts, using fairly thick cables to evoke ropes. Such a plan allows for the best integration of buildings with the site.

Moreover, in the bright sunlight of the region, this type of structure creates effects of light and shadow that recall those of the sliding panels of Japanese dwellings and suggest an interpenetration of interior and exterior.

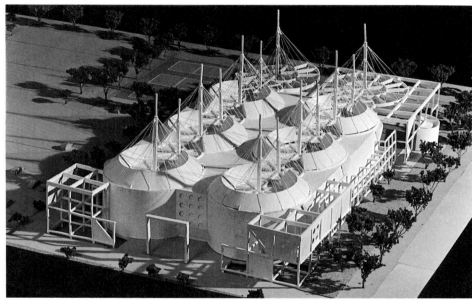

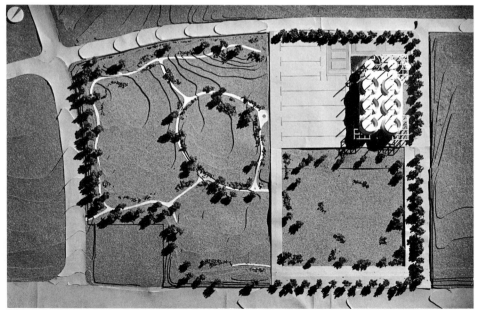

Thammasat University
Rangsit, Thailand, 1985

46 *Two floors.*
Structure: *Reinforced concrete.*

The Japanese Studies Institute, located north of Bangkok, was established as an auxiliary body of Thammasat University to promote Japanese studies in Thailand. The design aimed to create an authentically Japanese ambience while making the best use of local materials and construction methods. The attempt was also made to adapt the architecture to the local climatic and cultural conditions, taking into consideration function and ease of maintenance. The institute also had to be integrated into the overall scheme of the new campus of the university.

The layout of the institute draws on that of ancient Buddhist architecture (*Garan-haichi*) and Japanese palatial architecture (*Shinden-zukuri*). Four main buildings, each with a different function,

South facade.

48 surround an inner courtyard. The rear facade of the west buildings opens onto a Japanese garden, in which a tea house is located. By walking around the landscaped garden, one reaches the library and hostel buildings to the north and south, respectively.

The main entrance hall, located in the east building along with the administrative offices, is connected to the principal road by a bridge that crosses an artificial pond. Seen from the road, the buildings seem to be floating on the still water, creating a monumental effect.

On the exterior the buildings present a basic grid pattern with hollow block infill and a 45-degree sloped roof. The grid structure, a traditional design element in Japanese architecture, acts as a screen to filter the harsh sunlight and provide protection from violent rain. The sloped roof plays the same role of protection from the elements. Also, the small pipes that punctuate it at regular intervals release the radiant heat accumulated in the triangular space under the roof.

The exterior facade is almost entirely covered with terrazzo, either smooth and polished or rough and unfinished, an effect achieved by washing. This finishing work attests to the attention given to climatic and cultural conditions; the desire to integrate local construction methods led to the incorporation of regional materials into the project.

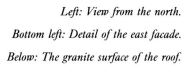

Left: View from the north.

Bottom left: Detail of the east facade.

Below: The granite surface of the roof.

Below: The Japanese garden.

Right, bottom, and opposite page: The covered walkways surrounding the courtyards.

SYMBIOSIS
OF PAST AND PRESENT

52 Modern architecture is marked by its rejection of historicism and styles of the past. Gropius and Le Corbusier deemed this a necessary rupture for various reasons. First, they felt a need to free themselves from the academicism of the Ecole des Beaux Arts, which then reigned supreme over European architecture. Second, they felt that modern architecture should make use of the materials and technologies of modern industry and turn its back on traditional craftsmanship.

The modern movement aligned itself with the aesthetics of abstractionism; these aspects together fashioned the modernist sensibility. It is easy to understand how Bruno Taut discovered in Japan, in the imperial villas at Katsura and in the two sanctuaries at Ise, justification for many of the elements basic to modern architecture. In the surfaces of bare untreated wood, the pure geometry of line, and the extreme sobriety of ornamentation, he would have perceived a modernist rejection of history. The rejection of history and ornament resulted in the so-called international style, which was supposed to cross all geographical and cultural boundaries.

I have often compared that process with the invention of Esperanto, a completely artificial language created by a synthesis of the various Romance languages. Its partisans hoped to achieve a universal culture, which depended on the negation of all linguistic, cultural, historical, and geographical disparities. In my view, the principles underlying the international style are totally analogous.

I began to have doubts about its legitimacy in the early 1960s. I suggested a metabolist architecture built on diachrony and synchrony, diachrony being a symbiosis of the past, the present, and the future. I went on to emphasize the need for modern architecture to remain in touch with the culture and history of a given region. However, we have to define what we mean by history. It can be "visible" history, manifested in architectural forms, ornamental motifs, and symbols inherited from the past; or it can be "invisible" history, that of states of mind, ideas, religions, aesthetic sensibilities, and ways of life.

In the West, history means the visible traces of the past. It seems to me that in Japan we give greater importance to the invisible things handed down from generation to generation. Thus the shrines at Ise, which for century upon century have been rebuilt every twenty years. Although the intent each time is to rebuild them in their original purity, there are inevitably modifications of details and furnishings, so that we can no longer accept the existing shrines as exact copies of the "originals." And yet the aesthetic principles in effect from the beginning have been perpetuated for more than a thousand years. In contrast, many ancient Western buildings still have their original materials but have long lain in ruins. In the West, history is preserved materially; in the East, it is preserved in the spiritual patrimony. During the Second World War some Japanese architects built concrete apartment houses topped with traditional Japanese tiled roofs.

In fact, that was a typically European thing to do. Since then, other architects have tried to make contact with history by recreating the styles of the past. With very few exceptions, such attempts have ended in failure. If we want to transcribe history in material objects, we would do better to begin by breaking it down into signs and symbols and incorporating certain of them into a modern work, where they could take on a new meaning. That is the method I used for the National Bunraku Theater. After having selected elements from the Edo period (the turret, the design of the doorknobs, etc.), I purified them in order to integrate them more happily into a modern structure. This procedure enables us to introduce tangible historical signs into modern architecture and, in so doing, to achieve a symbiosis of past and present.

Another method would be to reconstitute the atmosphere of the past, to impregnate modern architecture with the Japanese aesthetic, with Buddhist spirituality or traditional philosophy. The symbiosis thus achieved is with an invisible past, and the architect must discover a way to give a modern expression to an ancestral spiritual heritage.

A motif borrowed from the eaves of a sixteenth-century pavilion.

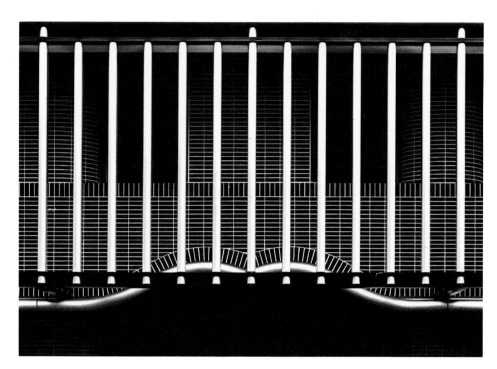

54 **Seating capacity of theater:** *753.*
Seven floors, two below grade.
Structure: *Steel rinforced concrete.*
Exterior: *Porcelain tiles; prefabricated
aluminum panels for the latticework gallery.*
Cost of construction: *$25 million.*

This building, located in the cradle of
bunraku (one of the traditional forms of
Japanese puppet theater), forms a com-

Perspective drawing of the facade.

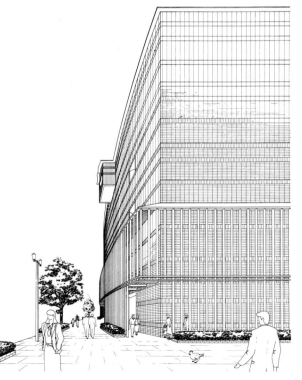

prehensive complex of related facilities,
including the main theater, a training in-
stitution, and archives of historiographic
materials.

As the program called for a theater
with a minimum capacity of 750 people,
the site, in a very crowded area in the
center of Osaka, was clearly too small for
a facility conceived along conventional
lines. The main theater was therefore
placed on the second floor, where the largest floor area could be obtained, relegating
to the first floor the entrance hall, exhibition areas, the cafeteria/restaurant, the
ticket counter, access to parking, and
areas for set installation. To facilitate access to the theater, the main staircases
and escalators leading from the first to
the second floor were placed in a large
atrium.

The main theater occupies four levels,
between the second and fifth floors. A
smaller hall with 159 seats, to be used as
a rehearsal and studio space, is provided
on the third floor. Lecture rooms, classrooms, conference rooms, administrative
offices, and storage areas are located on
the fourth and fifth floors.

The aesthetic conception of this building is based on a symbiosis of tradition
and modernity. Essential elements of the
traditional architecture of the Edo period,
carefully extracted and analyzed, are re-
ferred to throughout the design in the
form of abstracted symbols. These can
be seen in the Chinese-style curve of the
eave over the entrance; in the turret at-
tached to the upper part of the main facade (which recalls those once used to
announce performances); in the grid pattern on the ceilings and floors; in the lat-

56 ticework of the handrails; in the window around the lobby staircase, inspired by godown structures; in the design of the doorknobs in the auditorium, taken from the imperial villas of Katsura; in the black band and the horizontal cladding on the auditorium walls; and in the doors to the auditorium, which evoke traditional theater gates.

A projection at the second-floor level allows the full area to be utilized, providing a latticework veranda-like space underneath that surrounds the entire building. This treatment, in which an intermediate zone is created where external and internal spaces interpenetrate, recalls the veranda spaces under the roofs of traditional houses.

The requirements of a traditional bunraku performance are accommodated with the latest technology available today in the theater: the most advanced mechanical and electrical engineering is used in the design of the stage and associated areas. On the other hand, the furniture, including the auditorium seats, is designed to reflect the folk art that reached its culmination in the Edo period, drawing on the typical patterns of kimono fabrics.

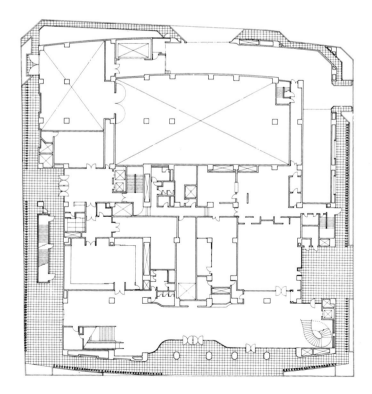
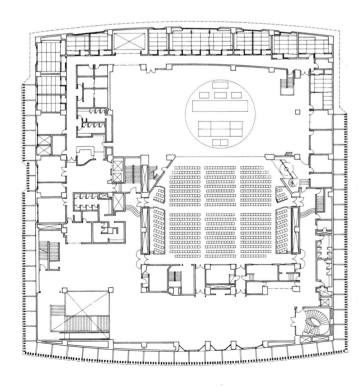

The cladding on the interior walls and the fabric of the seats are both inspired by the traditional styles of the Edo period.

Opposite page, far left: Window on the lobby staircase.

Left and below: The second-floor foyer.

Following pages: The principal facade; the curved eave above the entry; the turret.

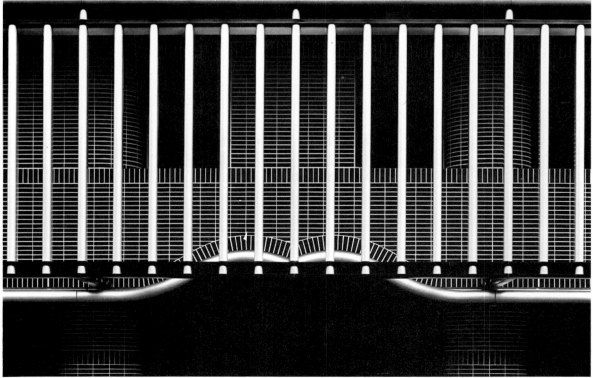

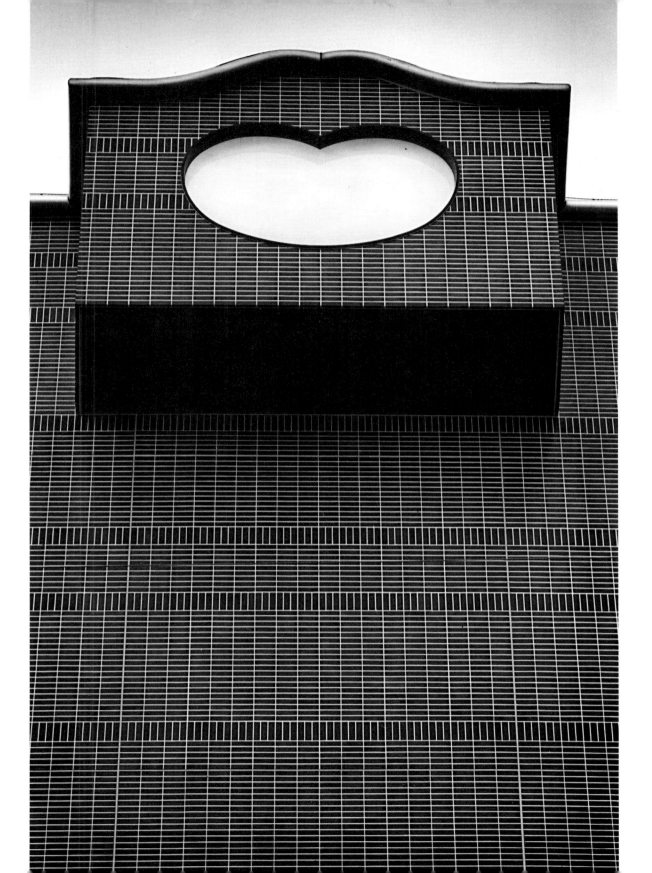

Fukuoka, 1984

62 *Fourteen floors, three below grade.*
Structure: *Steel reinforced concrete.*
Exterior: *Aluminum panels and glass.*

This corporate building, situated in the heart of Fukuoka City, is characterized by the simplicity of its design and by the incorporation of traditional Japanese elements.

The entire ground floor is occupied by a dry garden of white sand, stepping stones, and a sculpture, inspired by the celebrated rock garden of Kyoto's Ryoanji Temple. The exterior also evokes traditional architecture, such as the *engawa* and elements of the *sukiya* and *shoin* styles. The entrance thus creates an inviting atmosphere suitable to the image of the company.

The windows on each floor are inclined 9 degrees off the vertical to limit the penetration of sunlight in the summer.

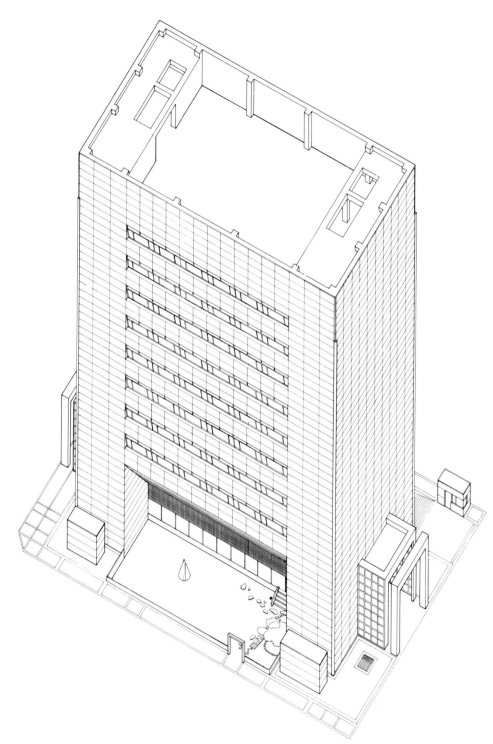

Isometric drawing.

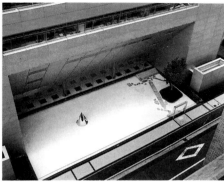

The dry garden.

Below: Transverse section.

Right, top: Perspectival section.

Right, bottom: The dry garden viewed from the street.

Opposite page: The lobby.

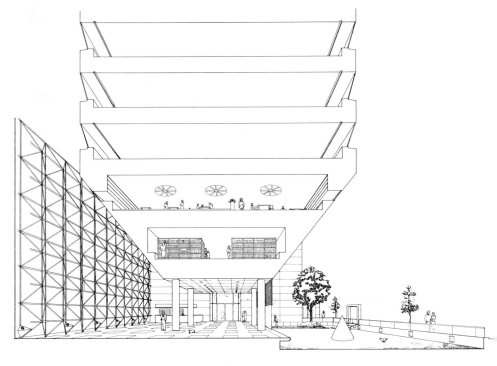

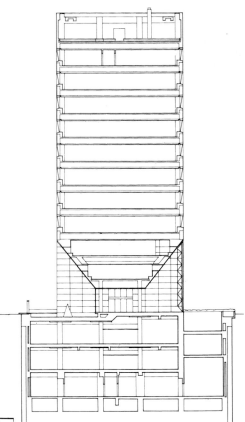

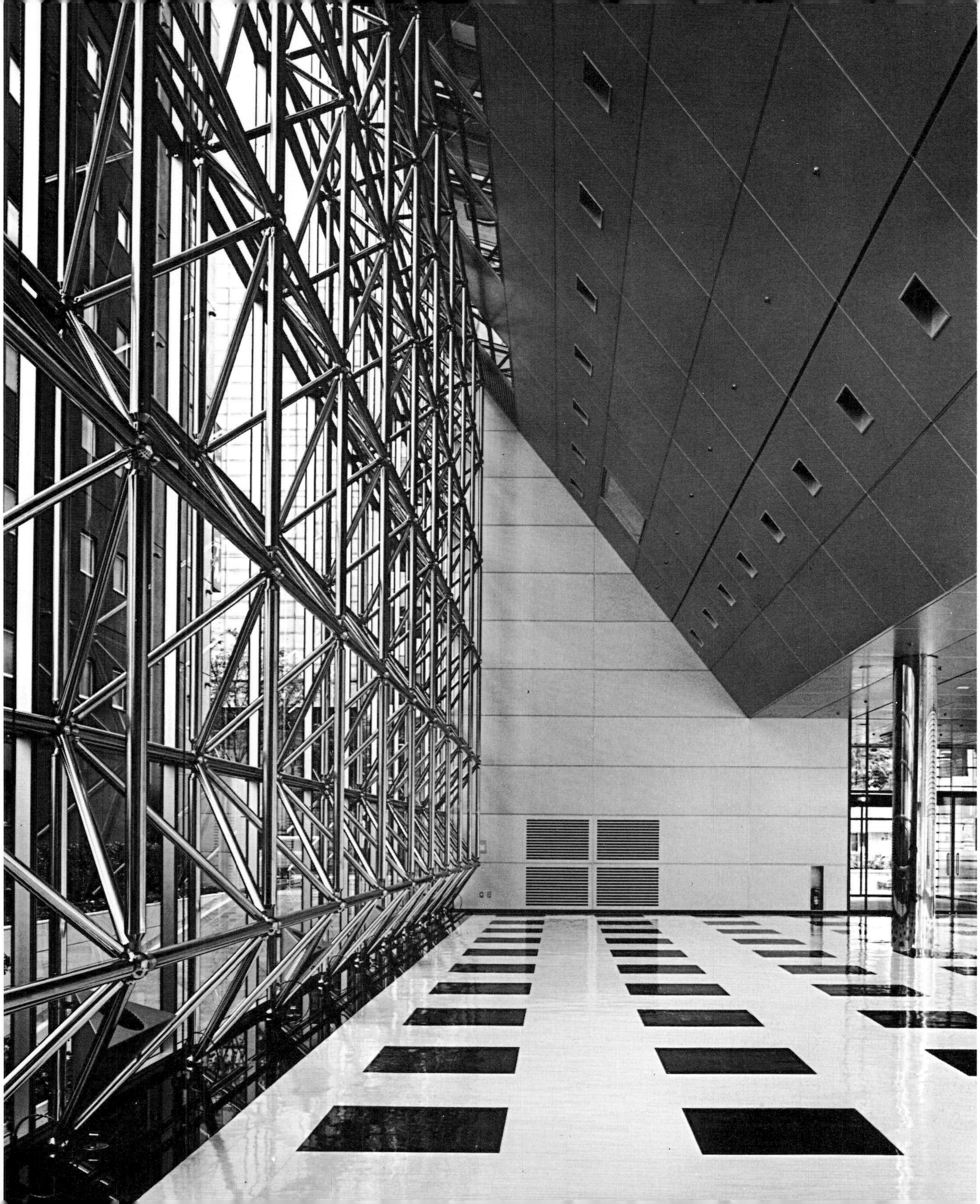

SARNATH YOSHIUNDO BUILDING

Niigata, 1985

66   *Five floors and a basement.*
Structure: *Reinforced concrete to the fourth floor; composite construction on the fifth floor; steel frame for the roof.*

This is the headquarters of a company that manufactures Buddhist altars. The president of the company, committed to spreading the message of Buddhism, wanted to do more than merely construct a building for the sale and display of his products. He wanted to build a structure that would be useful to residents of the area, which lacks cultural facilities, as well as conveying the religious message of the company.

In addition to the central showroom for altars and other Buddhist paraphernalia, the multipurpose complex includes halls, conference rooms, Japanese-style rooms of various sizes, a tea room, a gallery, a restaurant, and other facilities. The site is part of a larger compound that also holds the old headquarters, a factory, and warehouses. The area is adjacent to a national highway. Private residences and a public road border one side of the lot, where building heights are restricted to allow for maximum light. One of the main objectives of the design was to use these various constraints to the best advantage.

The shape of the lot and the various features of the facility led to positioning the complex perpendicular to the highway. The main entrance is located on the north side, adjacent to the parking lot. It is carved out of the building on all three above-ground levels, among other reasons, to control the amount of natural

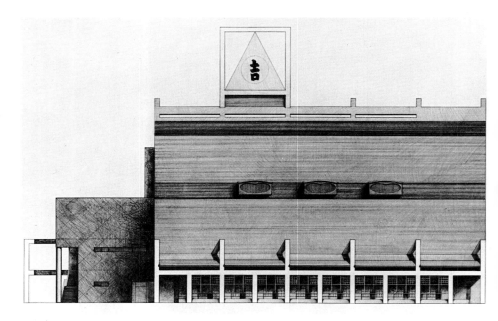

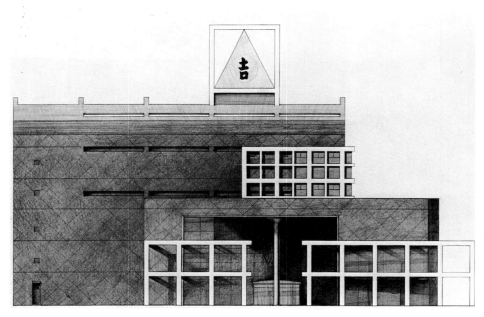

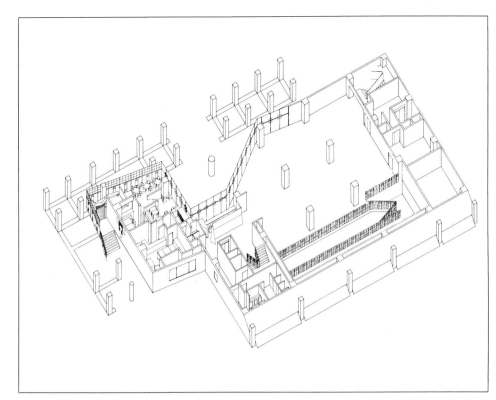

68 light entering the three-floor showroom where the products are displayed. This open space was designed to provide visual continuity between the showrooms and the lounge, the restaurant, the bar, the gallery, and other areas.

To create an intermediate zone between exterior and interior, a large light purple pillar was installed in the entry and the approach to the entrance was articulated by a three-dimensional lattice that brackets the structure on the north and the west.

The tea room, on the fourth floor, is a direct quotation of the Bosen tea room of the Kohoan at Daitokuji in Kyoto. A multipurpose hall with a seating capacity of 400 is located on the fifth floor.

The lowest level of the west wing forms an angle of approximately 7 degrees to the core of the building due to the shape of the site. The first floor of this wing is occupied by an exhibition space, the second floor by an Italian restaurant and a bar, and the third floor by a gallery. An exterior stairway, part of a "subentrance" to the building, leads directly to the wing's second floor; thus a sort of second facade is created, offering an important means of access to the complex.

The long line of the roof on the south side refers both to the line of the road and to the massive roofs of Japanese *minka* (traditional folk houses). Together with the three-dimensional lattice, this roof is one of the main features contributing to the unique character of the

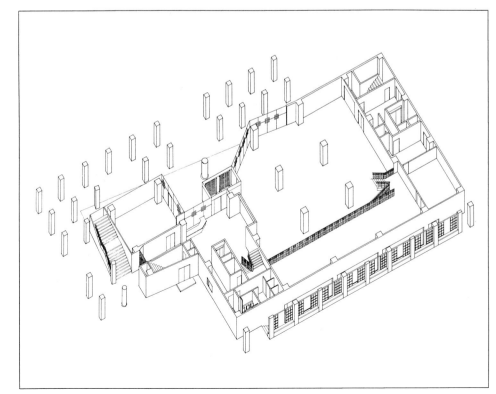

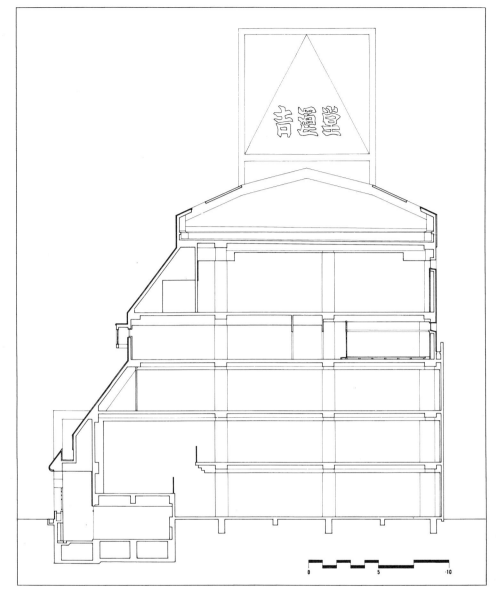

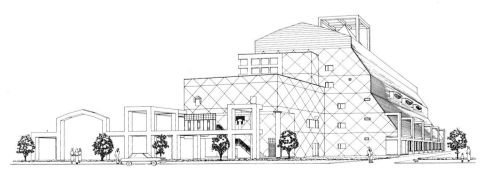

building. The projecting windows are 69 meant to suggest smoke vents, while the small structure on the roof evokes the old-style Japanese watchtower (*yagura*) or lantern (*andon*).

The underground space on the south side was requested by the client. The aluminum bars that separate this area from the exterior recall *shoji* sliding doors.

The exterior of the building, covered with aluminum and with black-and-white tiles, creates an effect similar to that of *namako heki*, which is created with square tiles and raised mortar. For the first time in Japan, lead siding has been used for the roof. The pillars, the beams, and the three-dimensional lattice have been given a silver metallic finish to complement the aluminum curtain wall.

Traditional Japanese colors have been used for most of the building: light purple for the large pillar, Chinese red for the sliding lattice doors and decorative windows, and pine green for the window and door frames and the stairway railings. The interior is predominantly white, with ash, navy, and purple accents. The furniture in the lounges on each floor, also in traditional colors, was designed especially for this building.

The basic philosophy of the design is a symbiosis of old and new, achieved by combining modern architectural techniques and materials with elements and details from the vocabulary of traditional Japanese design.

Details of the sales area and of the stairs leading to the second-floor restaurant.

Berlin
International Auction House, Special Mention, 1981

72   *Seven floors and a basement.*
Structure: *Reinforced concrete.*

The auction house was created for the International Building Exhibition organized by the city of Berlin. It addressed the problem of restoring an area situated between Friedrichstrasse and Charlottenstrasse, south of the "new town" of Friedrichstadt, built outside the city walls in the eighteenth century by Friedrich Wilhelm I. The scheme proposed preserving the existing building and re- creating the course of the old town ramparts.

Part of the new street facade is of latticework; the buildings are turned toward the interior and laid out around an irregularly shaped garden. There are thus two lines of facades: the "supple" facade corresponds to the diversity of activities to be carried on inside, while the "rigid" one camouflages that diversity in order to better integrate the renovated quarter into the town plan.

The latticework and the monumental door of the street facade link the interior garden with the exterior environment. Between the two, a transitional zone allows interpenetration between street space and the space of the building itself. Apartments, stores, offices, public facilities, and reception centers for the elderly and the handicapped are organized vertically, situated on different levels. Reflective materials on the facades introduce an additional spatial dimension and evoke an invisible world, as if through a looking glass.

Model, north facade; street elevation.

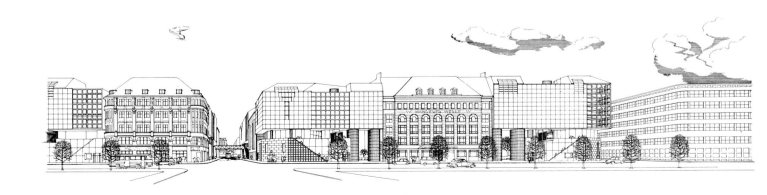

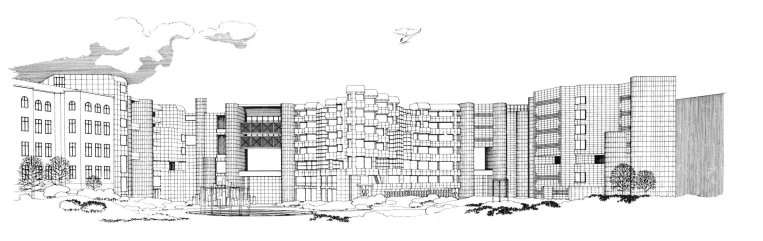

Isometric drawing.

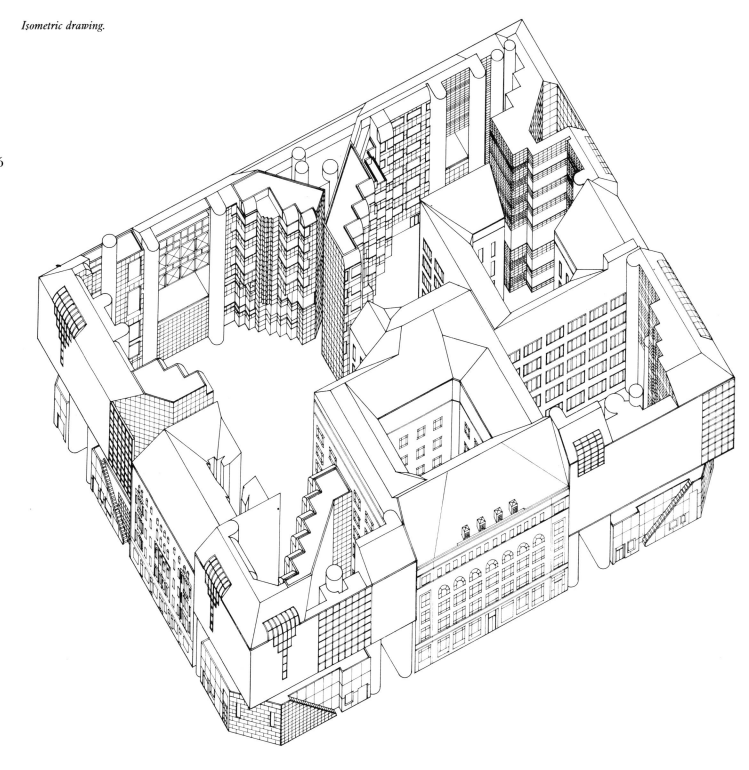

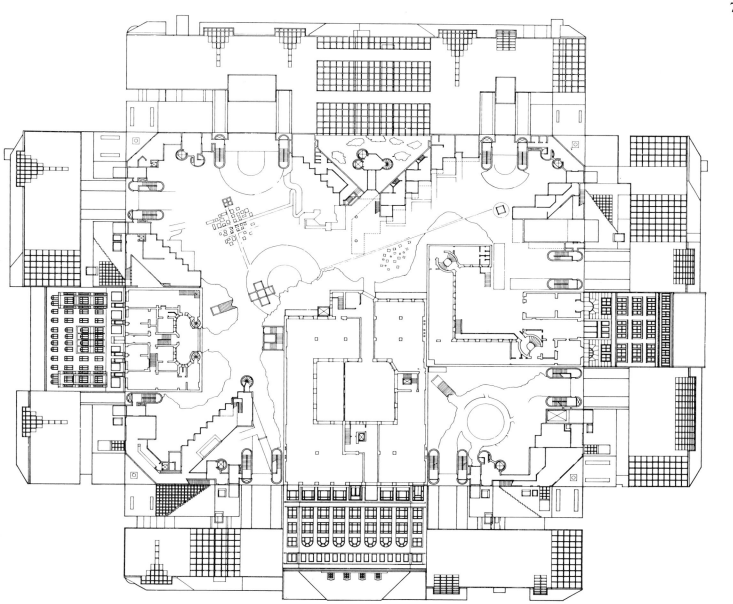

JAPANESE-GERMAN CULTURAL CENTER

West Berlin, 1988 (expected completion)
Co-Architect: Taiji Yamaguchi

78 *Four floors and a basement.*
Structure: *Reinforced concrete.*
Associate Architect: *Taiji Yamaguchi.*

The former Japanese Embassy in Berlin was constructed between 1939 and 1941 in the Tiergarten district. The architects responsible for the building design, Mashamar and Pinnau, worked under the direction of Albert Speer, director of Berlin's city planning under the Third Reich. Two years after completion, the building, damaged by bombing, ceased to be used.

It was not until 1970 that the city of Berlin began to discuss a plan to preserve the building, one of the few remaining examples of 1930s architecture. In 1980 the city submitted an official request for the restoration of the building to the Japanese government. At the same time, to commemorate Berlin's 750th anniversary, the city was preparing the International Building Exhibition, for which some 30 architects, from Germany and elsewhere, were invited to propose designs for the redevelopment of neighborhoods and the restoration of important buildings in the city.

The preliminary studies for restoration of the former Japanese Embassy were part of this program. The Germans, represented by the exhibition organizers, requested that the front facade be preserved because of its historical interest as an example of the transition between the styles of the Weimar Republic and the Third Reich. They also hoped for an integration of contemporary architecture. The project presented here was designed to satisfy these requirements while also offering the facilities necessary in a cultural center: a library, conference rooms, exhibition spaces, etc.

The series of front gates represents a fragmentation of historical, linear time. A section of the interior flooring has been opened up, and references to Schinkel have been inserted. The exterior and interior of the building incorporate quotations of Bauhaus designs. The central courtyard evokes Japanese Zen-style gardens. Thus, the restoration of the embassy is not a mere reproduction of the building as it stood during the Third Reich but rather a project that depends on diachronicity, in spanning the period from Schinkel's time to today, and synchronicity, in reconciling the two very different cultures of Japan and Germany.

Isometric drawing.

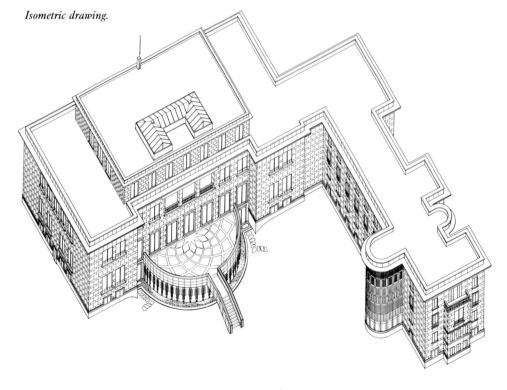

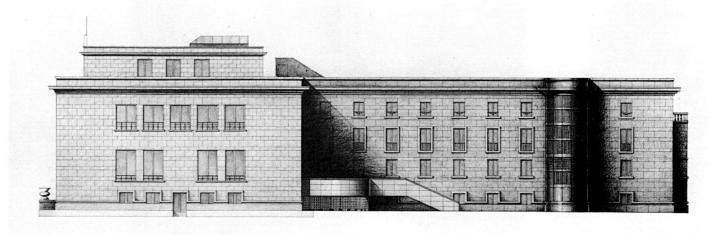

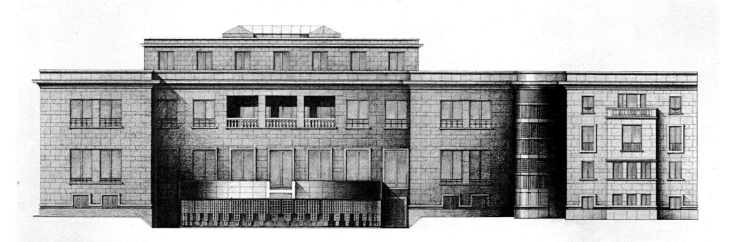

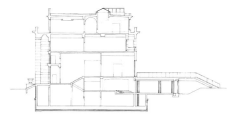

Transverse section.

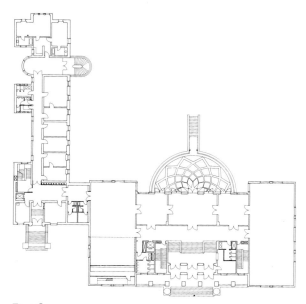

First floor.

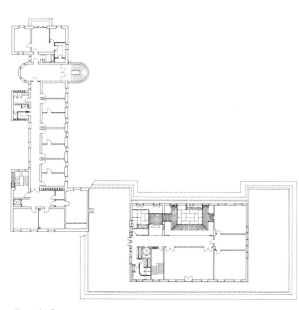

Fourth floor.

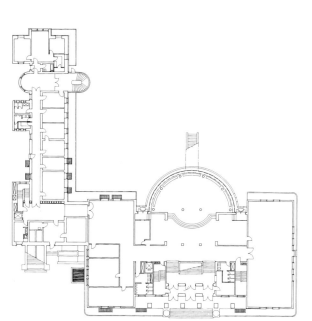

Second floor.

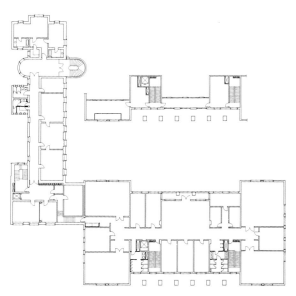

Third floor and mezzanine.

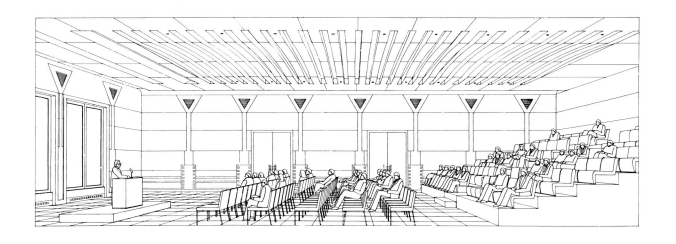

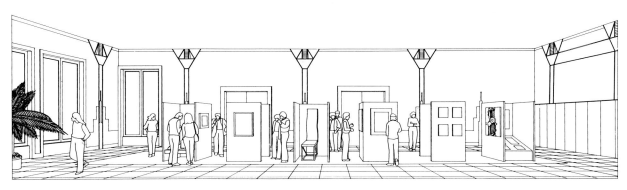

The lobby area on the first floor.

The multipurpose room on the second floor.

REDEVELOPMENT PROJECT

For Central Sofia, Bulgaria
Restricted International Competition, First Prize, 1983

Six floors and a basement.
Structure: *Reinforced concrete and steel.*

The 300-by-400-foot Serdica Complex is in the heart of Sofia's central district, adjacent to the Party Headquarters, Tum Department Store, City Hall, and Lenin Square (where Lenin's statue stands). More than half the site is occupied by commercial and public buildings and medium- and high-rise housing. This site is bounded by the ruins of the west gate of the old castle walls, within which it is located. Serdica was the ancient name of Sofia, dating back as far as Roman times.

The construction of subway lines is under way in the city; two lines cross at the southeast corner of this site, where a connecting station and underground concourse will be built.

To achieve a symbiosis of old and new buildings, this plan calls for the incorporation of structures from the seventeenth century through the first half of the twentieth century that are of particular historical value and can withstand repairs. This interplay with new buildings gives the whole a new life.

In consideration of the city's historical norms and traditions, the street pattern implicitly controlled by the existing city

East elevation.

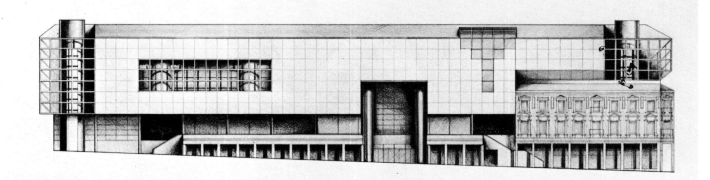

84 center was respected, as was the height of existing buildings.

The numerous courtyards found in the central city buildings inspired the idea of varying the scale of shopping areas, restaurants, hotels, etc., setting them apart from the atriums of the main entrance and plaza. A large roof was added over the west gate ruins to protect them from the very cold winters.

Aluminum, stainless steel, and protective glass were used as finishing materials in inconspicuous places, subtly highlighting the coexistence of old and new.

Isometric drawing.

VICTORIA CENTRAL

Melbourne, 1991 (expected completion)

86 *Seventy-five floors, two below grade.*
Structure: *Reinforced concrete.*

This building complex, located in the central business district of Melbourne, will comprise offices, retail space, and multiuse entertainment facilities. The high-rise (73-story) skyscraper in the complex will be the tallest commercial office building in Australia and probably in the entire Southern Hemisphere.

The nineteenth-century Shot Tower that stands on the site will be preserved inside a large glass cone, which forms an atrium at the center of the shopping complex and serves to symbolize the symbiotic relationship of past and present.

The office tower follows the tradition of skyscrapers designed as crystal-cut volumes. But within the overall smoothness of the building profile, the facades are made of such heterogeneous materials as stone, aluminum panels, and reflective and tinted glass.

High-technology communication equipment will be visible at the top of the tower, while the base of the building will be more traditional in conception. The building's facade represents a transition from the solidity of urban structures to the airiness of the sky.

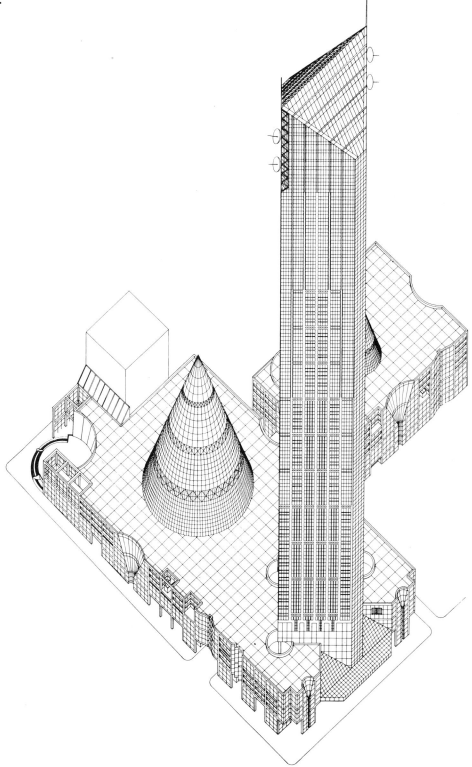

Isometric drawing, and model (opposite page).

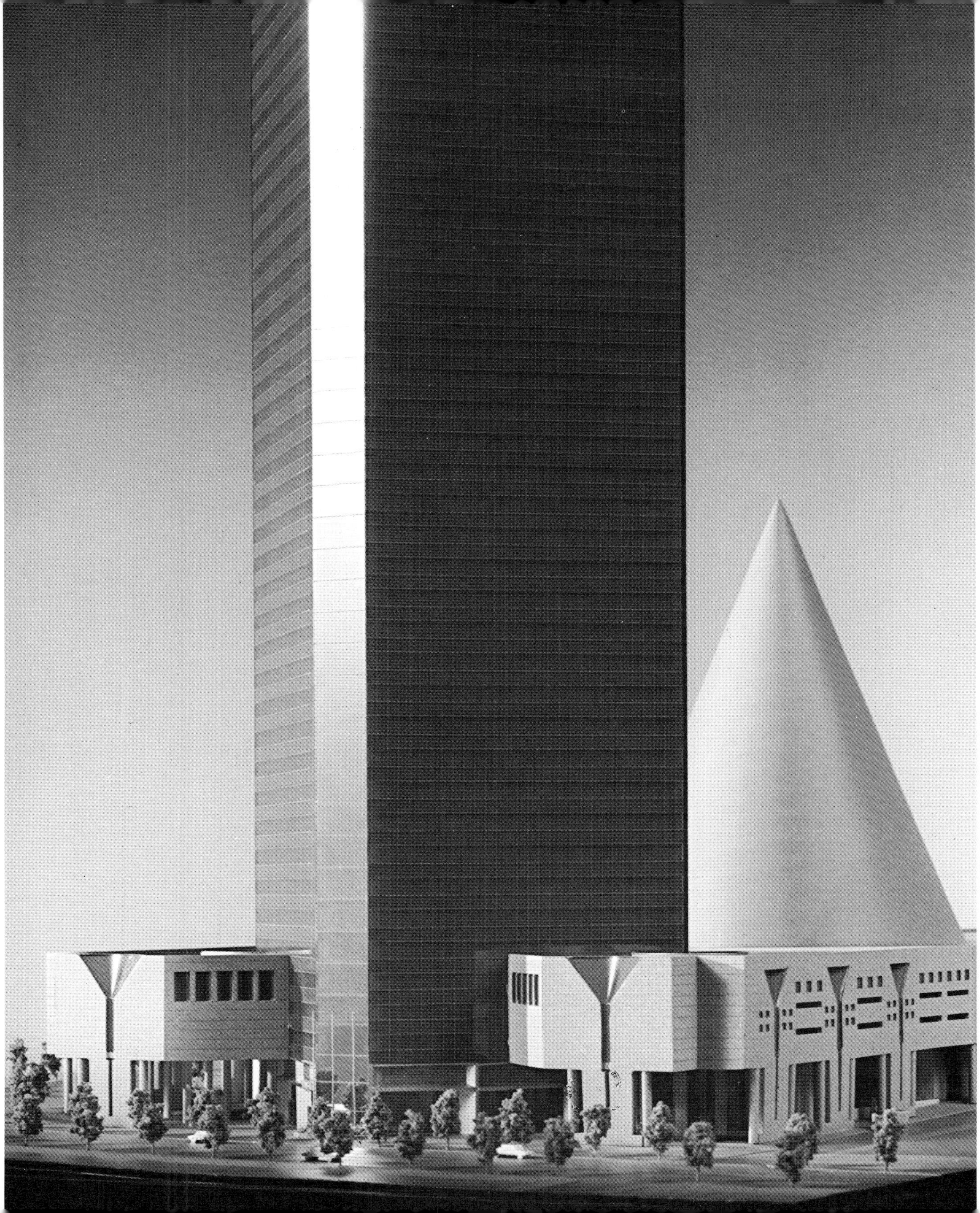

EL FATEH UNIVERSITY

Faculties of Architecture, Geology, Mathematics, and Physics
Tripoli, Libya, 1984

88 *Seven floors, one partially below grade, two below grade.*
Structure: *Reinforced concrete.*

El Fateh University (formerly Tripoli University), located 3 1/2 miles south of Tripoli, is the largest in Libya, with a student body of 25,000. Since the revolution of 1969, enrollment has increased dramatically every year, and all the departments have had to expand. This plan is for the enlargement of four departments within the College of Engineering—architecture, geology, mathematics, and physics. Under the university's new master plan, these departments have been alotted their own site and will no longer be housed in the old Engineering Building. The physics, math, and geology faculties will be located in one block, and the architecture faculty will be set off on its own.

The roof of each building, distinctive from afar, symbolizes the various functions of the structures. The asymmetry intentionally introduced in certain parts disrupts the overall symmetry of the plans.

Space is divided into two large areas, classrooms for the students and research and administration areas for the faculty. Architecturally, they are two clearly separate volumes, but they intersect in a plaza conceived as a place for the exchange of information between students and faculty. Respect for Libyan traditions and research into natural ventilation led to the inclusion of courtyards in the design.

The latest technology was put to use in this project: solar energy, water purification, and computer-controlled environments. Also, the use of precast concrete elements shortened the construction time.

Isometric drawing.

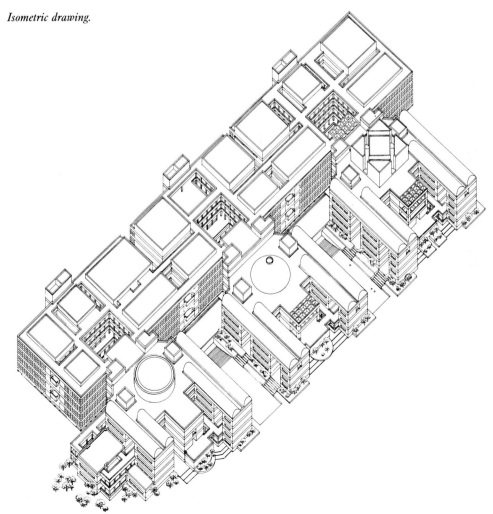

Top: North elevation and west elevation.

Bottom: Plans of the first and fourth floors.

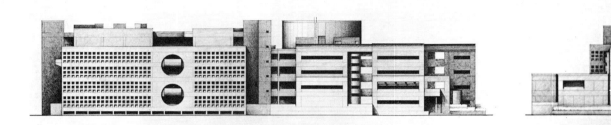

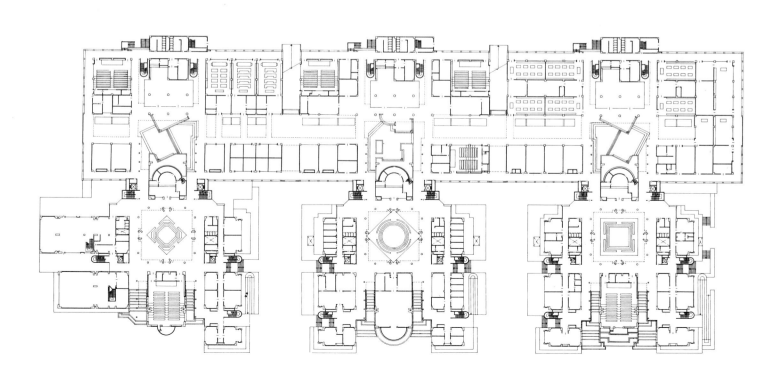

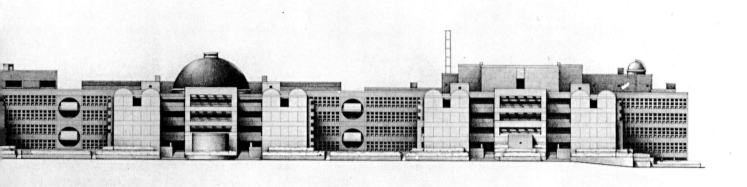

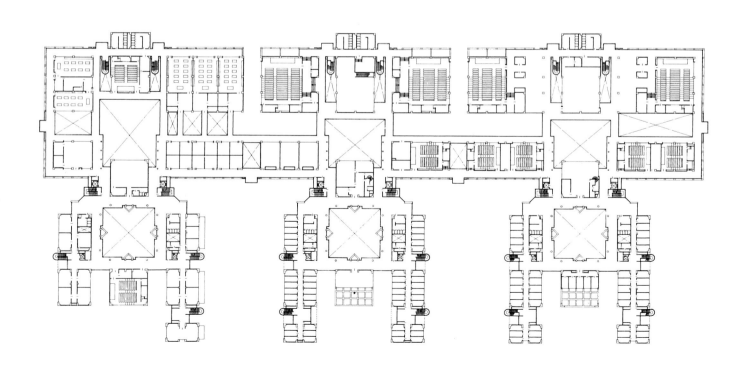

92 Prior to Claude Lévi-Strauss's structuralist analyses, it was commonly held that cultures had achieved different degrees of evolution. In that schema, European (and especially French) culture occupied the highest echelon. Then came the cultures of the Americas, of Japan, and of the underdeveloped or developing countries of Africa and the Middle East. The theory of economic growth elaborated by Walt Whitman Rostow was conceived along the same lines. The American economist discerned several stages, from the primary economies of traditional societies to the full maturity of the consumer society. From this perspective, "progress" for an economy or a culture meant progress toward the Western model, to the point where, for the majority of countries involved, modernization became synonymous with Westernization. And, indeed, that is the course upon which many nations, including Japan, embarked.

The year 1868 marked the beginning of the Meiji period, during which time Japan began to try to modernize and Westernize itself. That vast undertaking affected every sector, from industry to education, justice, and architecture. Western-style buildings came to be the symbols of modernization. The "world-view" ideal preached the progressive Westernization of all countries, which would lead to the creation of a perfectly homogeneous planetary culture based on Western values. The linguistic instrument for that culture's establishment was to be Esperanto, and its architectural instrument the so-called international style. That pure product of Western culture was to become a universal icon.

It was architecture with a capital A. Architectural modernism boiled down to a determination to propagate the "more highly evolved" Western culture worldwide under the banner of the international style.

The underlying evolutionary principles involved are still at work. We find in the desert, in the steaming jungles of Southeast Asia, and even in China the same glass boxes that we find in Manhattan.

Synchrony, which is one of the two great principles of metabolist architecture, is an indictment of the modernist doctrine. This is one of the fundamental tenets of structuralism. Lévi-Strauss demonstrated that every culture has its own characteristics that create a system with all other cultures at any given moment. Put another way, Western culture should not be viewed in terms of a linear development but in terms of its relationship with the world's other cultures. Lévi-Strauss relativized the notion of cultural "superiority" and recognized each culture's legitimate place in a multidimensional worldwide reality. There is the same distance (or closeness) between Japanese culture, for example, and Islamic culture or European culture. The universal icon of modernism was shattered to bits, and we became free to create an architecture nourished by many different civilizations. The new syncretism rests on the principle of cultural equi-distance, which I believe is the essential condition for passage from the international style to the multicultural style toward which we are now moving.

The movement was already under way in the early 1960s with metabolist architecture's affirmation of synchrony.

In Yokohama, the symbiosis of Japanese and
Western architecture is fully realized.

WACOAL KOJIMACHI BUILDING

Tokyo, 1984

Nine floors and a basement.
Structure: *Steel.*
Surfaces: *Artificial marble and aluminum veneer.*

The new Tokyo headquarters of the Wacoal Company, a lingerie manufacturer, had to be a multipurpose space, capable of functioning as a creative studio, a business office, a display area, and a new product warehouse. It also had to take into account Wacoal's expansion into the production of such other clothing lines as nightgowns and outer apparel. Markedly different from most corporate architecture, this building has functions and meanings that overlap and intermingle. Storerooms serve as display areas, displays areas as studio spaces, and studio spaces as offices. The whole of the building functions as a universal space, making it a kind of empty signifier.

As a creative center for the fashion industry, it represents an observatory through which one can peer into the future of haute couture. This role is underscored by a series of visual "stimuli" that serve as indications of what lies ahead. Among the more prominent is a white wall behind the main facade showcase that shapes itself around reliefs by Issey Miyake, striking simulacra of the naked human form. The awning extending over the main entrance suggests a flying saucer, a brief visitor from the world of the future, while on the wall that greets visitors as they enter, a mirrored stainless steel sculpture by Minami Tada casts a distorted reflection from the past. In front

South facade.

Detail of the south facade.

96

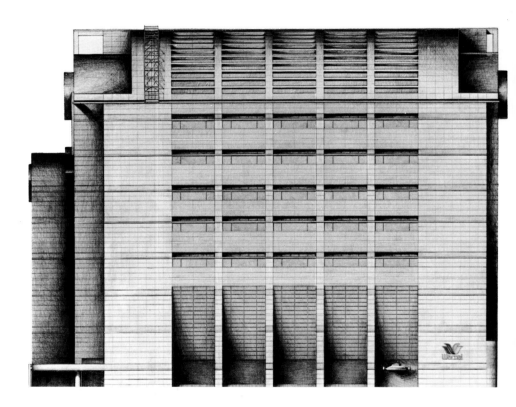

of the elevators, the floor depicts an age-old geomantic symbol in a mosaic of marble gathered from the countries along the Silk Road.

On the ninth floor, the reception room overlooking the Imperial Palace is a spaceship with Japanese décor; its telescope-window reproduces part of a traditional astrological chart from the *Ensai Kansho Zusetsu*, published by Yoshio Shunzo in the year Bunsei 9 (1826). Lighting elements in the ceiling repeat the auspicious "eight directions" of the geomantic symbol, while the *fusuma* (sliding doors) and the decorative bracketing are reminiscent of Kyoto architecture. We exit this timeless setting through a facade à la Della Porta that lends a surprisingly smooth note of counterpoint. Proceeding down to the seventh-floor meeting room, we find a smaller telescope-window patterned after the *Botai Hanpi-Zu* (Chart of Divisions and Opposites) by the Edo-period philosopher Baien Miura.

These and other signs—referring to the future, referring to a past as far back as the Edo period—bring together the most far-flung aspects of Japanese culture to participate in a vast diachronic performance that inspires in us a synchronic *plaisir du texte*.

The ceiling lights of the ninth-floor reception room.

Below: The director's office, on the eighth floor.

Bottom: The ninth-floor reception room.

98

Lighting integrated into the pillars and walls of the exhibition room on the sixth floor.

The wall of the ninth-floor reception room, and the hallway that leads to it.

ROPPONGI PRINCE HOTEL

Tokyo, 1984

Capacity: *221 guest rooms.*
Nine floors and a basement.
Structure: *Composite (steel and reinforced concrete).*

This innovative hotel, located in the popular international district of Roppongi, is designed to serve as a salon. To take full advantage of the site's limited size, the building is organized around a central courtyard; the perimeters of the building extend to the outer limits of the site. In the courtyard is a swimming pool and a heated terrace. Around them are grouped a sauna, a coffee shop, an exercise room, and restaurants, to encourage year-round use of the area as a kind of salon. Details from various cultures and various times are incorporated as hidden signs of "simulacra" to evoke humor and conviviality.

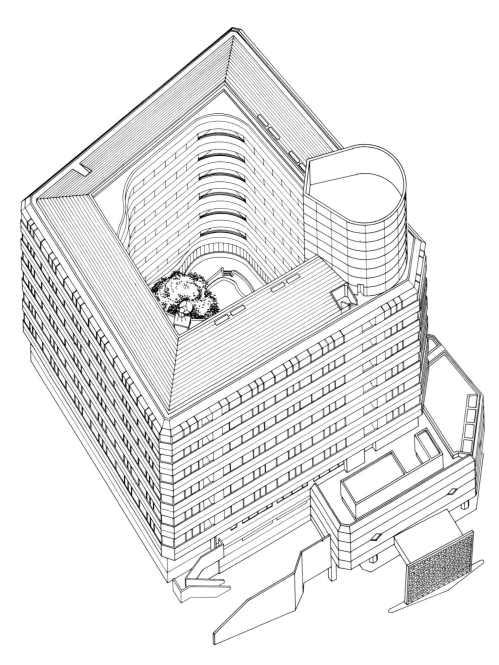

Isometric drawing.

Second floor.

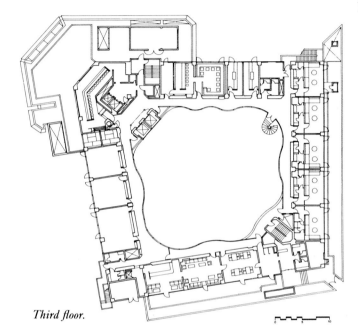

Third floor.

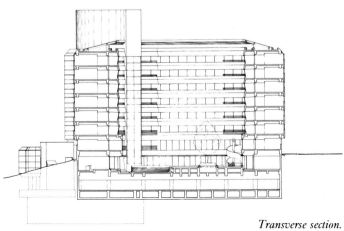

Transverse section.

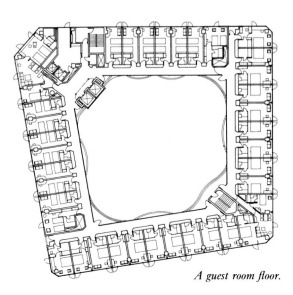

A guest room floor.

104

The swimming pool.

The tempura snack bar.

Opposite page: The "classical" bar and restaurant on the second floor.

106

Below: A guest room.

Bottom: The entrance to the sushi restaurant.

Opposite page: The staircase of the entry hall.

Toyama, 1986

110　*Seven floors and a basement.*
Structure: *Composite (steel and reinforced concrete).*
Exterior: *Aluminum panels and ceramic tiles.*

In every prefecture in Japan is a facility like the Koshi Kaikan Center, a structure built for the mutual-aid associations of public-school teachers. This building is situated in the center of Toyama, about 450 yards from the station, and is surrounded by roads that form the pentagon-like shape of the site.

Designed to serve as both a reception facility for the educational community and a hotel, the building is open to the general public and stands out as a city landmark. The plan incorporates elements associated with Japanese iconography and East Asian cosmology in general.

Consider the circular hotel tower resting on a square base. Square and circular motifs predominate throughout the building, overlapping and distending at certain points to create a dynamic effect. The tower roof is a loose interpretation of the steep-pitched rooflines typical of the traditional architecture of Toyama, where it snows quite heavily. The use of iconographic elements that refer to distinct cultural contexts is, in a sense, a way to "acclimate" the architecture.

The building is made up of two parts: a "high-rise" portion for the hotel accommodations and a "low-rise" portion for the mechanized parking lot. The high-rise is oriented toward the station, with the main approach located on the northwest corner to accommodate the majority of hotel guests who arrive from the station. A lounge occupies the center

West elevation.

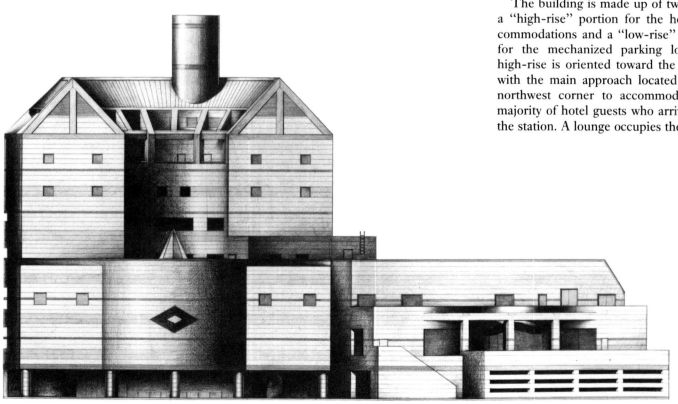

of the first floor. From there, part of the 111
triangular roof of the high-rise can be
seen, creating a feeling of openness in
the limited space. On the north side of
the lounge is a multipurpose gallery, an
open exhibition space set off by a glass
wall.

On the second floor are three conference rooms: one large, one medium, one
small. The first two can also be used for
parties; the third is strictly for confer-
ences. To the west is a small auditorium
with 300 seats that are movable, making
the space adaptable to the various needs
of the users.

A large and a small conference room
are located on the third floor. Both rooms
have a style that blends Oriental and
Western influences. The third floor of the
low-rise portion of the building holds a
wedding hall, accompanied by a beauty
salon and a photo studio.

The fourth and fifth floors, with Japanese-style rooms only, are reserved for
hotel rooms and dining rooms. The
fourth floor opens onto a terrace that can
be used as a playing field for gateball
games and other sports.

The seventeen rooms on the sixth floor
are designed in four different styles.
The director's room faces Tateyama
Mountain.

The seventh-floor restaurant also has a
view of the mountain. A fiber-optic system and a film projector transform the
ceiling into a sky full of stars and clouds,
an image that creates a bright atmosphere
in the restaurant, regardless of the
season.

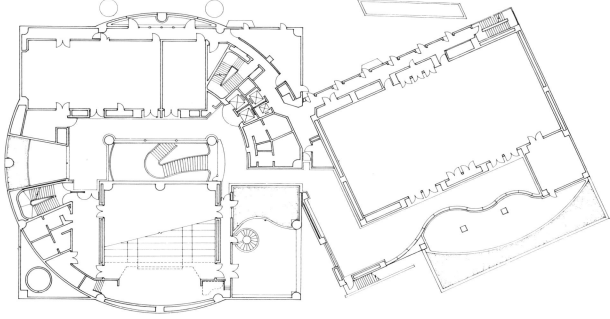

First floor.

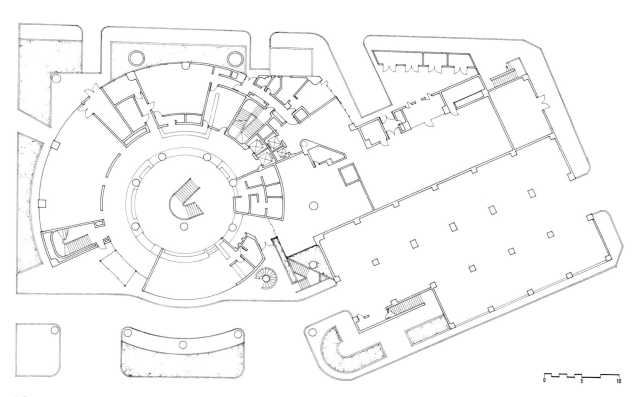

Second floor.

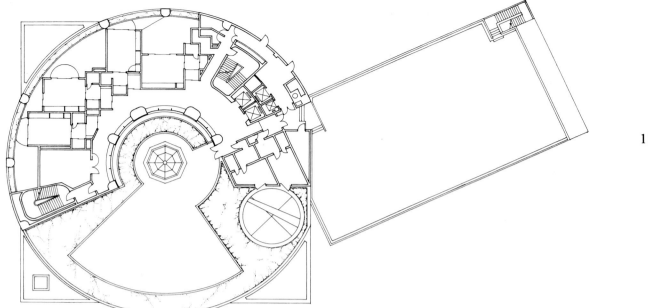

Fourth floor.

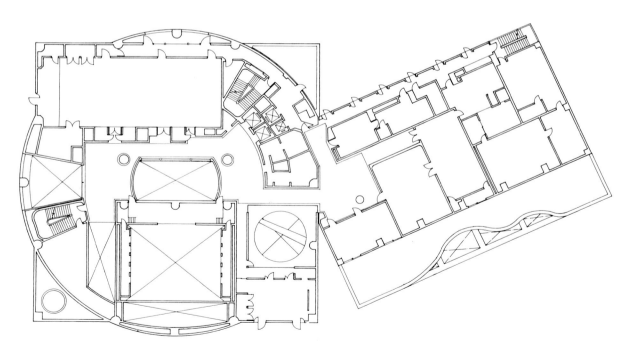

Third floor.

114

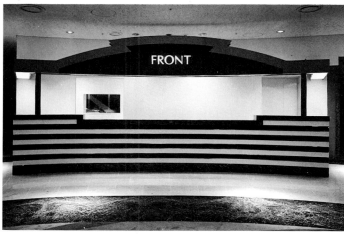

FRONT

Yuki, 1986 (first phase)

116 **Laboratory building:** *Three floors, one below grade, and a penthouse.*
Administration building: *Five floors, two below grade and a penthouse.*
Structure: *Reinforced concrete.*

In 1978 the Bayer Company, based in Leverkusen, Germany, sponsored an international contest for the design of a plant quarantine research center. The Kurokawa plan was awarded first prize. Construction began the next year in Düsseldorf and is now nearing completion. While this project was under way, Nihon Tokushu Noyaku Seizo, which is affiliated with Bayer, decided to build a similar facility in Yuki (Ibaraki Prefecture). In 1985 the administrative building was completed. This phase of the project also included a technical building.

Though the Yuki research center is only one twentieth the size of the Bayer center, the aim was to employ the same basic design features and concepts.

The laboratory building has three stories. The top floor contains the climate-control apparatus; regulatory mechanisms are located in the basement. The primary goal here was for maximum flexibility in the future.

Below: The administration building.

Opposite page: The laboratory building.

Hiroshima, 1988 (expected completion)

118

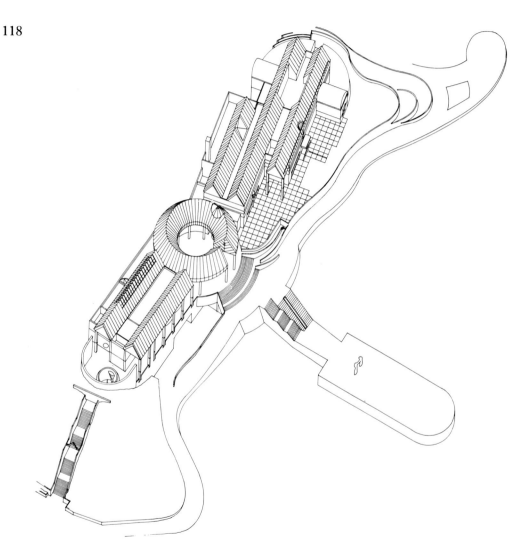

Four floors, two below grade.
Structure: *Reinforced concrete and steel reinforced concrete.*

This project represents the first public museum in Japan to declare contemporaneity its exclusive goal. In Hiroshima the contemporary period is that following the atom bomb. For a city that has eradicated from memory its entire prewar history, the term "contemporary" has a particular depth of meaning, forging a link between art and peace. Cities everywhere, not only in Japan, are searching for their identity and wondering how to build an image for the future. In Hiroshima this image is constructed around the idea of international peace; indeed, the city has little else on which to build its identity, other than its geographic location on a delta. In consideration of these aspects, this project has a very particular importance.

The site is atop a hill 150 feet above the city that bears some resemblance to the Acropolis in Athens. It is a cultural center known as the Hijiyama Art Park, a 75-acre area that, according to Kurokawa's master plan, will also include a science museum and a library. The whole is surrounded by the greenery of an ancient nearby forest that completely shuts

it off from the noise of the city. There are pedestrian paths completely separated from automobile routes, a sculpture park, an outdoor school, open areas, nature walks, etc. The care taken with every detail shows the attention given to the needs of everyone, from toddler to senior citizen.

The museum itself encompasses 100,000 square feet, large by Japanese standards. To preserve the beauty of the site as it is seen from the city, 60 percent of the space is below ground; the building becomes, in effect, the roof of the hill. With its length exceeding 660 feet, the building includes many staircases to facilitate circulation, elements that also create a more artistic space.

The building is oriented along axes determined by the other facilities, all of which converge in the round plaza in its center. Because much of the building is below ground, earth has been removed at points around the structure, and large openings have been created to alleviate the enclosed feeling in the lower levels.

The design of the roof and walls of the building refers to the traditional Japanese *kura* (warehouse) of the nineteenth century. As for the materials of the facade, the combination of stones, tiles, and aluminum adds to the impression of various periods in symbiosis.

East elevation and south elevation.

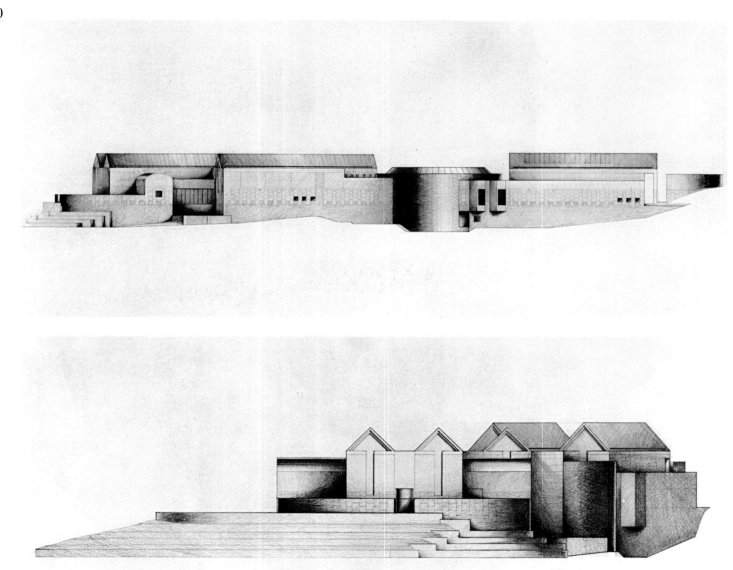

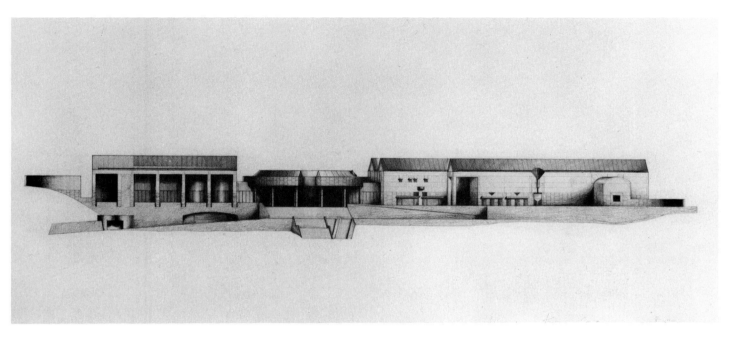

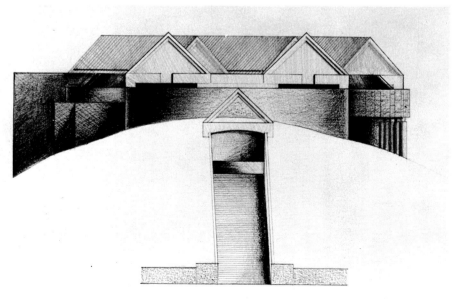

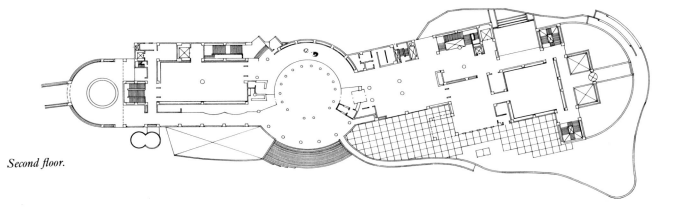

122 *Second floor.*

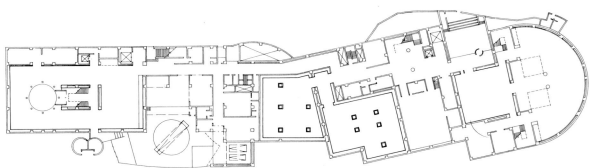

First floor.

First basement level.

Second basement level.

0   10   20

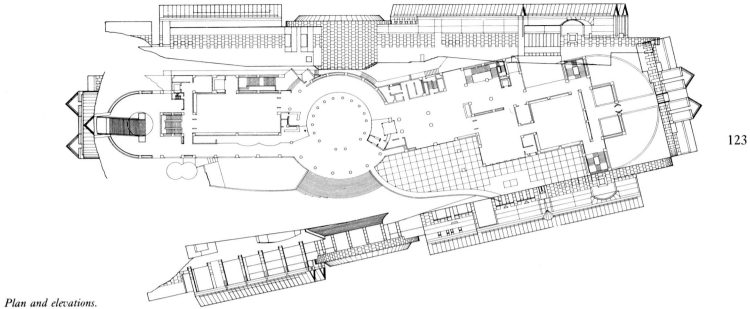

Plan and elevations.

Transverse sections.

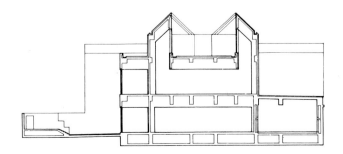

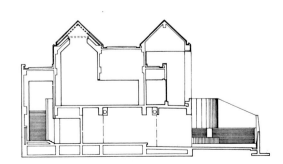

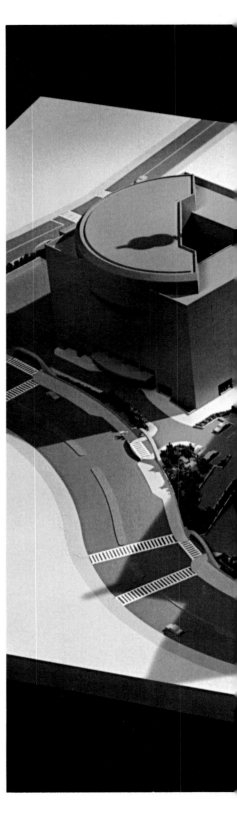

124 **Administration building:** *Sixteen floors, two below grade, and a penthouse.*
Parliament bulding: *Six floors, one below grade, and a penthouse.*
Police headquarters: *Nine floors, one below grade, and a penthouse.*
Structure: *Composite (steel and reinforced concrete) for the lower floors; steel for the upper floors.*

The construction of this huge complex, including an administration building, a parliament building, and a police headquarters, has been planned to permit the optimum use of the existing buildings on the site while the new buildings are being completed. In order to integrate the complex into the overall context of the Naha cityscape, the whole site is landscaped in a harmonious combination of straight and curved lines, with the rich greens of the area. A central courtyard is provided in each building to provide natural lighting and to allow for ventilation in the tropical weather.

A variety of different materials, including stone, terrazzo, tiles, aluminum, and titanium, are used on the facade, creating the effect of a textile that interweaves past and future. The silhouette of the roof is inspired by those of traditional village houses.

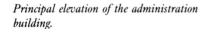

Principal elevation of the administration building.

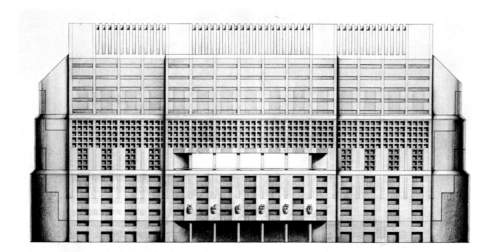

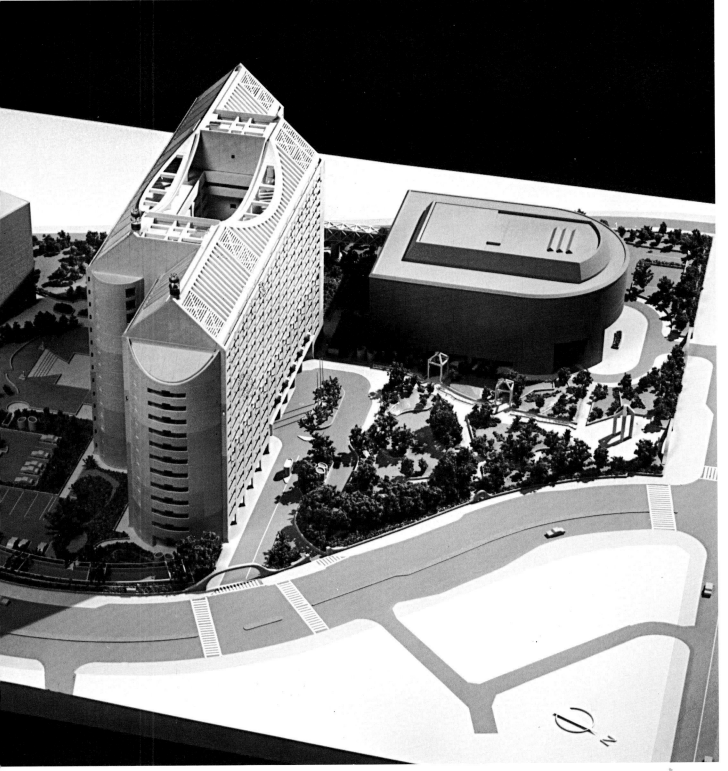

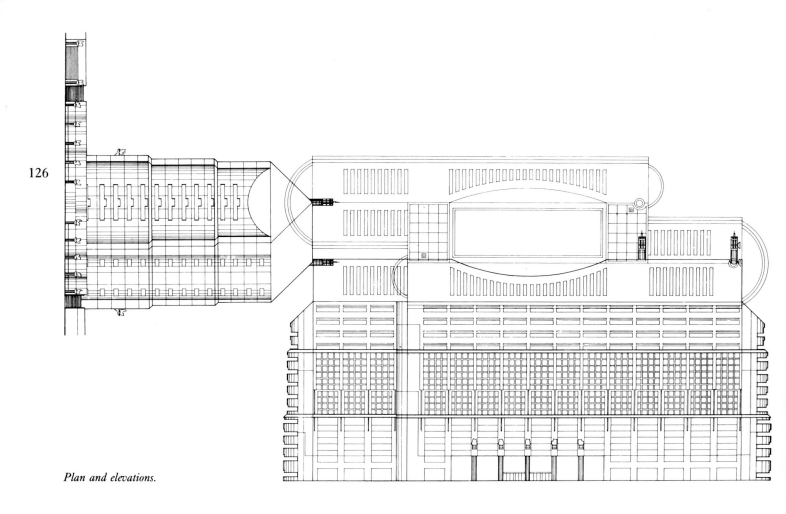

Plan and elevations.

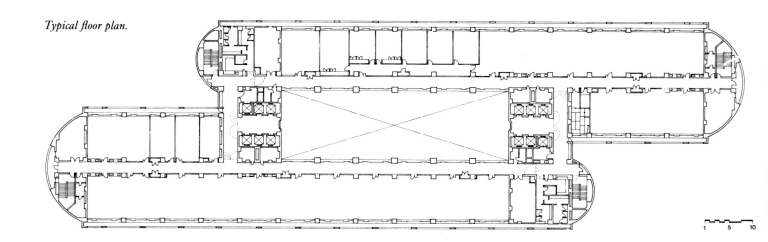

Typical floor plan.

1 5 10

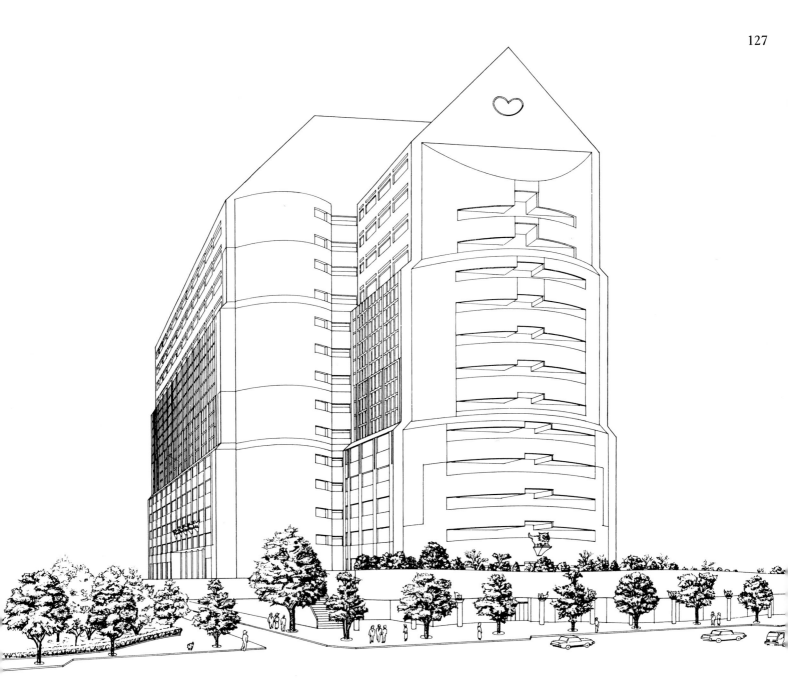

Nîmes, France
Study, 1985

128 **Housing and hotel:** *Eight floors.*
Offices: *Five floors.*
Structure: *Reinforced concrete.*

This residential and office complex would serve as a gateway between the central city of Nîmes and the southern sector, now under development.

Arranged in a half-circle along the Boulevard Allende, a major traffic artery into the city center, the structure would be penetrated by the avenue Jean-Jaurès.

Its configuration recalls the celebrated arenas of Nîmes, dating from the Roman era, and thus represents a metaphor for the entire city. The half-arena shape is made up of five concentric semicircular parts.

The circle of trees located in the center of the traffic circle symbolizes nature; the pedestrian bridge that surrounds it symbolizes the notion of linkage. The arc of the office building symbolizes the industry of Nîmes; that of the pedestrian mall symbolizes the cultural and commercial activities of the city; and that of the residential units, located at the outside limit, symbolizes habitat.

These five metaphorical arcs are arranged to gradually become lower toward the center, clearly evoking the levels of an arena.

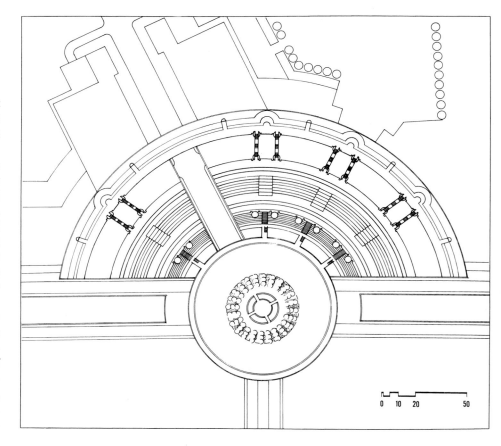

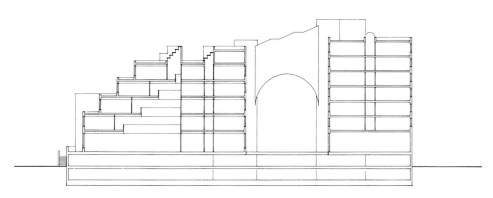

Site plan and transverse section.

Top to bottom: North elevation, south elevation, and perspective drawing.

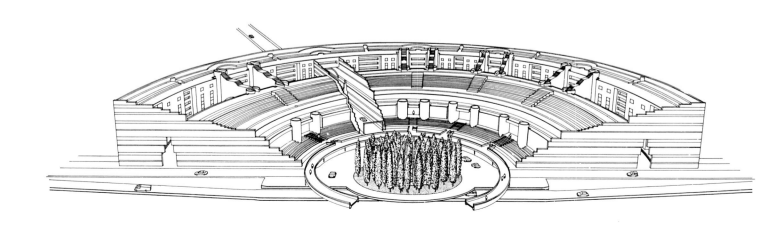

Detail of the sports center.

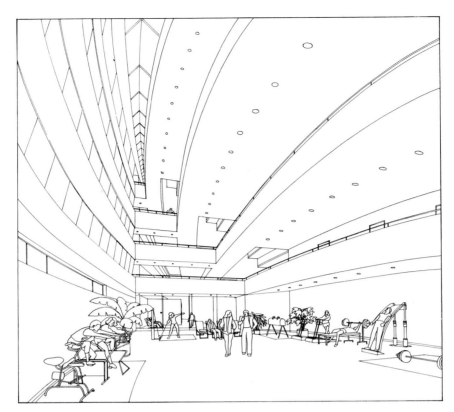

The pedestrian promenade.

132

1960 Project for an agricultural town.
1961 Grand spiral project for Tokyo.
Project for the Kasumigaura neighborhood in Tokyo.
1962 Project for prefabricated cube apartments.
Nishijin Social Center, Kyoto.
1964 Nitto Food Co. Cannery, Sagae.
Children's park, Andersen Museum, Yokohama.
1965 "Metamorphosis" project.
Central pavilion, children's park, Yokohama.
1966 First project for the new town, Hishino.
First project for a center for the handicapped, Aichi.
1967 New town, Fusijawa.
City Hall, Sagae.
Hawaii leisure centers, Yamagata.
1968 Space Capsule discotheque, Tokyo.
1969 Project for a floating factory.
Odakyu drive-in restaurant.
1970 Toshiba and Takara pavilions for Expo '70, Osaka.
1971 Project for the Darmstadt Museum of Contemporary Art.
City Hall, Sakura.
Azabu House No. 2, Tokyo.
1972 Nakagin Tower, Tokyo.
LC–30X Leisure Capsules.
1973 Shimoda Prince Hotel.
Karuizawa Prince Hotel.
Capsule country house, Usami.
1974 Sports stadium and center, Vasto, Italy.
Urban plan for the Vasto region.
Big Box leisure centers, Tokyo.
Azabu House No. 1, Tokyo.
1975 Fukuoka Bank headquarters.
Daido Insurance company offices, Sapporo.
City Hall, Wakicho.
1976 Prefabricated concrete cube houses.
Sony Tower, Osaka.
Takahashi Residence, Kamakura.
Bell Commons headquarters, Tokyo.
Tateshina Club hotel and residences, Kitasaku.
Tateshina Club planetarium, Kitasaku.

1977 Ishikawa Cultural Center, Kanazawa.
Ethnological Museum, Osaka.
Headquarters of the Japanese Red Cross, Tokyo.
1978 Municipal Museum, Kumamoto.
Daido Insurance Company headquarters, Tokyo.
1979 Hotel Vitosa, Sofia.
Project for a spa, Acapulco.
Kyojuso Villa and tea pavilion, Hachioji City, Tokyo.
1980 Project for the new town d'As-Sarir, Libya.
Shopping arcade, Matsudo.
Shoto Club, Tokyo.
1981 Faculties of Architecture, Geology, Mathematics, and
Physics, El Fateh University, Tripoli.
Opera house and hotel, Khaskovo.
Concept for the Japanese exhibition, Royal Academy
of Arts, London.
Prefecture, Fukuoka.
Saitama Prefectural Museum of Modern Art, Urawa.
1982 Mechanical and Civil Engineering Institute, El Fateh
University, Tripoli.
Advanced Institute of Banking and Management,
Tripoli.
"Edo" furniture line.
1983 Mutual Insurance offices, Yokohama.
National Bunraku Theater, Osaka.
Toranomon Hospital, Tokyo.
Municipal Agency of Commerce and Industry, Nagoya.
Hiroshima Municipal Museum of Contemporary Art.
Skyscraper and cooperative buildings, Kuala Lumpur.
Redevelopment project for central Sofia.
1984 Wacoal Kojimachi Building, Tokyo.
Yasuda Fire Insurance Building, Fukuoka.
Roppongi Prince Hotel, Tokyo.
"Edo" line of furniture: table and armchair.
Okinawa Prefectural Government Headquarters, Naha.
Koshi Kaikan Center, Toyama.
Central Plaza I, Brisbane.
Tourist lodgings, Hainan Island, China.
1985 Universal Exposition of Science and Technology,
Tsukuba: Foreign pavilions; pavilions for IBM, Toshiba,

and Mitsui; electricity and automobile pavilions.
Japanese Studies Institute, Thammasat University,
Rangsit.
Sarnath Yoshiundo Building, Niigata.
Nittokuno Research Center, Yuki.
Japanese-German Cultural Center, Berlin.
Victoria Central, Melbourne.
House for Sino-Japanese Children, Beijing.
Agency for Quality and Productivity, Sofia.
Ministry of Industry and Technology, Sofia.
Project for Rond-Point Nord, Nimes.
1986 Miki headquarters, Tokyo.
Newport Beach Sports Club.
Central Plaza II, Brisbane.

AWARDS

In Japan

Takamura Kotaro Prize (1965).
Signalment Association Prize
(1977: gold and silver medals, 1979,
1980).
Building Trades Prize (1977, 1978,
1979).
Hiroba Prize (1977).
Mainichi Prize for the Arts (1978).
Chubu Prize for Architecture (1978).
Prize for the Most Beautiful Storefront
(1978).
Office Architecture Prize (1985).

Elsewhere

Grand Prize in the Plastic Arts of Sofia
and Bulgarian Order of Merit (1979).
Commander, Order of the Lion, Finland
(1985).
Gold Medal, Academy of Architecture,
France (1986).

C O M P E T I T I O N S

1963 Congressional Palace, Kyoto.
National Theater of Tokyo.
1967 Hokkaido Centennial Monument, Sapporo, second prize.
1969 HLM pilot project for Lima (competition sponsored by the United Nations), first prize in collaboration.
1971 Georges Pompidou Center.
1972 National African Union of Tanganyika headquarters, Dar es-Salaam, first prize.
1975 Congressional Buildings, Abu Dhabi.
1976 International Hotel, Abu Dhabi.
1977 International Theater, Abu Dhabi.
Council Chambers, Abu Dhabi, third prize.
1979 Plan quarantine research center for Bayer, Mannheim, first prize.
1980 International Building Exhibition, Berlin; special mention.

S O L O   E X H I B I T I O N S

1981 Retrospective, Royal Institute of British Architects, London.
Drawings and woodcuts, Riccar Museum, Tokyo.
1982 Woodcuts, Ban Gallery, Osaka; Marronnier Gallery, Kyoto; Sakura Gallery, Nagaya.
French Institute of Architecture, Paris.
1983 National Institute of Architecture, Rome.
Advanced Institute of Architecture and Civil Engineering, Sofia.
1984 Salon Construma, Budapest.
Architects House, Moscow.
University of Kyoto.
Matsuya Department Store, Tokyo.
1985 Solo exhibition at the Architecture Biennale, Buenos Aires.
Institute of Architecture, Bucharest.
Finnish Museum of Architecture, Helsinki.

1986 Drawings, Kohju Gallery, Kyoto.
Collegium Artisticum, Sarajevo.
Museum of Architecture, Wroclaw.
Academy of Architecture, Paris.

G R O U P   E X H I B I T I O N S

1960 XII Triennale, Milan.
"Visionary Architecture," Museum of Modern Art, New York.
1961 Urbanism exhibition, Tokyo.
1962 "Metabolism," Tokyo.
1963 "Contemporary Japanese Architecture," Florence.
1973 "Capsule Architecture," Rome.
1974 National Institute of Architecture, Rome
1978 "Drawings of Visionary Architecture and Urbanism," New York.
1984 "About Michel Ragon," Paris Art Center, Paris.
1985 "Cities of the Future," Sao Paulo.

T I T L E S   A N D   A P P O I N T M E N T S

In Japan

Consultant to the Japanese Railroads (1970–1980).
Consultant to the Japanese Foundation (1972–1980).
Member of the Urbanism Commission, Ministry of Construction (1976–1980).
Member of the Teaching committee, Ministry of Education (1977).
Commentator on NHK Television.
Consultant to Prime Minister Ohira (1979–1980).
President of the First International Congress of Architecture and Culture, Yokohama (1980).
Member of the Federation of Professional Architects, the Association of Architects, the Institute of Urbanism, and the Institute of Architecture.

Elsewhere

Lifetime member of the Society of Arts, London (since 1976).
Honorary member of the Royal Institute of British Architects (since 1986).
Honorary member of the American Institute of Architects (since 1981).
Co-president of the International Congress of Architecture, Aspen, Colorado (1979).
Commissioner of the "Japan Today" exhibition, Chicago (1979).
Lecturer at the University of Beijing (1986).

CONFERENCES

Universities of Hiroshima and Tokyo, Technological Institutes of Nagoya and Hiroshima,
Chambers of Commerce of Tokyo, Osaka, and Sapporo.
Fujita, Asahi Shimbun, Toyota, Nomura, IBM-Japan, Nissan, Nippon Steel, Mitsui, Matsushita, Sumimoto companies.
Ministries of Exterior Commerce, Industry, Foreign Affairs, Justice, Education, Construction.
American Center, Kyoto, Osaka.
Architectural Assocation, London; Royal Institute of British Architects, London; Cambridge and Oxford universities; University of Tennessee, Yale and Columbia universities; Association of Bulgarian Architects; Union of Soviet Architects; Association of Sarajevo Architects; Academy of Architecture, Paris (1986); Secretariat of State for Tourism, Sofia . . .

MONOGRAPHS

In Japan

Nobel Shobo Editions (1969); Bijutsu Shuppan Publishing Co. (1970); Mainichi Shimbun Publishing Co. (1975); Kenchiku Goho (1979); Kajima Institute (1979).

Elsewhere

Royal Institute of British Architects, London (1981); Le Moniteur, Paris (1982); Electa, Milan (1983); Fratelli Fiorentino, Naples (texts by Lia Papa and Vicenzo Manocchio, 1984).

PUBLICATIONS

Numerous untranslated works on metabolist architecture, prefabricated houses, urbanism, the "hypertechnological" society, contemporary architecture, the media, the city, space, modern society. Certain texts or extracts have been translated for monographs published outside of Japan. Translations into Japanese: Jane Jacobs, *The Death and Life of Great American Cities* (1969); Charles Jencks, *Modern Movements in Architecture* (1976).

136 ILLUSTRATION CREDITS

Masao Arai: pp. 46, 47, 48, 49, 50, 51.
Tomio Ohashi: pp. 9, 13, 14, 23, 26, 27, 28, 29, 31, 33, 34, 35, 36, 37, 53, 54, 57, 58, 59, 60, 61, 63, 64, 65, 67, 70, 71, 94, 95, 96, 97, 98, 99, 100, 101, 104, 105, 106, 107 top, 108, 109, 111, 114, 115, 117.
T.D.R.: pp. 6, 17, 21, 30, 40, 41, 44, 45, 72, 73, 74, 75, 83, 87, 89, 107 bottom, 116, 119, 125, 132.

Cover photo: Masao Arai—Shinkenchiku.